2000 Mules

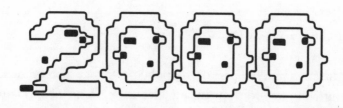

2000 MULES

THEY THOUGHT WE'D NEVER FIND OUT. THEY WERE WRONG.

THE FULL STORY

DINESH D'SOUZA

Regnery Publishing
WASHINGTON, D.C.

Regnery® is a registered trademark and its colophon is a trademark of Salem Communications Holding Corporation

Cataloging-in-Publication data on file with the Library of Congress

ISBN: 978-1-68451-083-2
eISBN: 978-1-68451-115-0
Library of Congress Control Number: 2022941095

Published in the United States by
Regnery Publishing
A Division of Salem Media Group
Washington, D.C.
www.Regnery.com

Manufactured in the United States of America

10 9 8 7 6 5 4 3 2 1

Books are available in quantity for promotional or premium use. For information on discounts and terms, please visit our website: www.Regnery.com.

For my daughter,

Danielle D'Souza Gill,

who brings wit, love, and joy to everyone around her!

Truth is incontrovertible. Panic may resent it. Ignorance may deride it. Malice may distort it. But there it is.[1]

—*Winston Churchill*

CONTENTS

Why the Truth Is So Important

What theft could be graver than stealing an election? This is especially true if you were stealing an election for the presidency of the United States, and control of the United States Senate. You would be stealing the government of the most valuable thing in the world, the United States of America. It would be the heist of the century, arguably the greatest heist of all time.

The big question, of course, is did it happen? Did the Democrats steal the 2020 presidential election? Did they steal the two Senate seats in the Georgia runoff? Did Trump win reelection? Is the wrong man in the White House? Was there a coordinated ring of election fraud large enough to tip the balance in these races? Or, conversely, was this the "most secure election in American history"?

Here are my answers. This was *not* the most secure election in history—far from it. I can show that there was a coordinated ring of election fraud more than sufficient to tip the balance in both the presidential race and in the Georgia runoffs. Further, I can show which side organized and pulled off the heist—the Democrats, working through an elaborate criminal network set up for this purpose.

Did Trump win the 2020 election? Yes, he did. Was it stolen from him? Yes, it was. Granted, this cannot be proven with Euclidean certainty, because there is no way now to ferret out the fraudulent votes and separate them from the good ones. They are all mixed in together. But we don't need *absolute* certainty to know with *reasonable* certainty what happened.

Trump won, and by a decisive margin, which is to say that absent the cheating, Trump would have won all the key swing states. Even the most conservative calculus—the narrowest way of reading the evidence that I will present—shows Trump winning the election. I'm less confident about Perdue and Loeffler, although there was massive cheating for the Democrats in those races as well.

I depicted these discoveries in my film *2000 Mules*, which quickly went on to become the most successful political documentary in a decade—indeed since my own first documentary, *2016: Obama's America*, which came out in the summer of 2012. This book will establish the case outlined in *2000 Mules* through more thorough documentation, evidence, solid math, and argument than can possibly make its way into a movie. It will also answer the "fact-checks" and objections raised against the film, mostly from the Left, but some from the Right as well.

There is one group of diehards reading this book who will respond, "I knew it! I was right. Now, Dinesh, can we drag Biden out of the White House?" I'm not sure about that one. We are in uncharted territory here. One view, of course, is that this is a fait accompli, a done deal. Legally all options have been exhausted. There was a narrow window for the Trump campaign and its allies to make and prove the legal case. This did not happen. So from this perspective Biden is here to stay, at least until he keels over or completely loses his mind or somehow runs out his term. For now, we're stuck with this guy.

But I don't want to jump too quickly to this conclusion, to concede the inevitability of Biden's remaining in office. If you steal a country, don't you have to give it back? Shouldn't the cheaters be deprived of the fruits of their criminality and corruption? The Constitution seems not to have anticipated the problem that we are dealing with here. The only specific remedy it provides for removing a president is impeachment. I discuss all this in my last chapter.

But let's assume for now that there is no way to get Biden out, and that to this degree the Democrats have gotten away with their heist. Hearing this, the diehard might erupt in exasperation, "In that case, Dinesh, what's the point of all this? What's the point of putting forward all this evidence when nothing can be done about it?" The point is to know the truth. Consider the case of a burglary or rape where the statute of limitations has expired. Legally, there is no way to lock up the perpetrator. Yet if there is DNA or other evidence that shows who did it, it is still good to know. Truth matters. If you felt in your bones that something went terribly wrong in the 2020 election, I'm here to tell you that you were right.

Even the protesters who went to Washington, D.C., on January 6, 2021, to let out a primal scream that no one was adjudicating the issue of election fraud, and to demand of their elected representatives that they pay attention to it and do something about it, were right. They were not part of any "big lie." In fact, they were there to challenge the big lie that this was the most secure election in history, that there was no systematic fraud involved in 2020, and that Biden won legitimately and decisively. Nothing could be further from the truth.

What happened in the 2020 election was a profound subversion of the democratic process. The very party that is now clamoring about "saving" and "protecting" democracy was involved in an organized scheme to undo democracy. Indeed, to a degree, they did undo it. And now they are doing their best to cover it up, with the full support of a compliant media that supports the heist and is even, in a manner I'll illustrate, in on the heist.

The digital platforms Facebook and YouTube are also accessories to the crime. (Twitter was too, but Twitter is a different animal since Elon Musk announced his takeover bid.) They censor content in the name of blocking "misinformation," but what they fear most is the truth getting out. When I released the teaser trailer for 2000 *Mules* I posted it only on Rumble. I didn't even post it on Facebook or YouTube.

That's not because anything in it was false. Remarkably, the trailer did not attract even a single fact-check. Nothing in it could be challenged, let alone disproven. Yet I couldn't upload it to Facebook or YouTube because the very suggestion of election fraud—even supported by video evidence—violates the explicit rules of these platforms and is automatic grounds for being shut down or banned. Remarkably, in our free society we are not free even to *talk* about election fraud.

Moreover, the Biden administration is using the judicial apparatus that has fallen into its hands to go after "election deniers." The Department of Homeland Security even lists those of us who question the bogus narrative of the "most secure election in history" as potential domestic terrorists. I expect I am already on their radar, and if by some oversight I am not, I will be once this book is published. They seem terrified the truth will come out, and, like any Third World junta, they are unleashing their goons to prevent that.

There have been a number of wild, unsupported allegations about the 2020 election. Consequently, I am likely to have a second type of reader in addition to diehards looking for vindication. This is the skeptic who says, "Here comes the latest conspiracy theory about how the election was stolen." Of course, this view comes mostly from Democrats, but it also strikes a chord among some Republicans.

This was the view adopted by Joe Scarborough on *Morning Joe* in response to the documentary. Scarborough made no effort to deal with the content of the film. He merely aligned it with previous theories and fretted that swatting each of the conspiracy theories down was an unending project of "whack-a-mole."[1] I'll discuss the issue of conspiracy theories later, but to a degree I can sympathize with this sentiment. It is a natural response to crazy things that have been said, theories that are impossible to validate and implausible on their face.

To such a reader I would say, "Forget everything you've heard so far. Forget everything that you 'know' about election fraud. I'm writing a book that doesn't rely on suspicions, hunches, or speculations. I'm not making a case for what could have happened. I am showing you, through evidence as reliable as fingerprint evidence and DNA evidence, what did happen. I cannot tell you the full story of the 2020 election because I don't know it. But I can tell you what I do know, and what I know is both decisive and damning, and comes with the largest conceivable implications for our future as a democracy. In the end, I'm confident you'll agree with me there was a heist, the criminals are still at large, and the party of the criminals is now running the country."

This might seem like a deeply depressing book. That is not my tone or approach. Rather, my approach is sober, investigative, skeptical, and analytical. Like a prosecutor making a case, I'll rely on various types of evidence. I will answer objections and candidly confess what can and cannot be shown. For me, this is a liberating enterprise because the truth is always liberating. I even find it exhilarating. I'll end the book by showing how the criminals can be held accountable—how satisfying it would be to see all of them in handcuffs—and how to prevent such a heist from occurring again.

CHAPTER 1

Why We Can't "Move On"

Elections are the lifeblood of a democracy. Modern democracy is based on the idea of representative government, a government "of the people, by the people, for the people." Elections are the mechanism by which the people choose who is going to rule on their behalf, in their stead, and for their interests and welfare. Without elections, there would be no way for the people to exercise their legitimate sway on the future direction of their country.

Admittedly there are many people who say the United States is not a democracy but rather a republic. When Benjamin Franklin was asked at the conclusion of the Philadelphia Constitutional Convention what form of government the founders had devised, he famously replied, "A republic, if you can keep it." Legal scholar Randy Barnett is typical of conservative and libertarian scholars who insist that the founders *rejected* democracy in favor of a republican system of government.[1]

Barnett points out that many of the founders spoke derisively of democracy as a form of mob rule. For the most part, however, they were speaking of ancient democracy—the democracy of Athens in the fifth century BC—which was direct and not representative democracy. In a direct democracy, there is no need for elections because the people themselves make decisions for their society; they don't have to elect others to do it for them. In ancient Athens, some twelve thousand or so citizens would show up in the agora or public square and decide, through majority vote, such important decisions as whether Athens should build a statue to a particular god or go to war.

Representative democracy, however, requires that people choose surrogates to govern in their place. Like direct democracy, representative democracy is based on the principle of majority rule. Some of the founders, notably Madison, harbored serious doubts about representative democracy because majority rule might give rise to the "tyranny of the majority." Majorities, in other words, could use their power to oppress minorities, another form of tyranny.

Consequently Madison, the chief architect of the Constitution, helped devise a system that limited the sphere of the federal government and combined majority rule with minority rights. The Bill of Rights enumerates "unalienable" rights that accrue to us as individuals (or to the sovereign states) and precede the existence of the federal government itself, so that even an elected majority cannot abridge or trample them; and the Constitution vests Congress with the power to establish courts to protect these rights.

None of this means, however, that the United States has an undemocratic system of government. On the contrary, we are a democracy, but of a particular kind. We are a *constitutional* democracy, which means we are a democracy that operates under the authority of, and through the mechanisms of, a written Constitution. The Constitution itself is not subject to majority revision, and it can only be changed by supermajorities in Congress and in the states through a process specified in the Constitution itself.

Within the tracks established by the Constitution, including the Electoral College, ours is a system of majority rule. At the national level, this means that the president, the members of the House of Representatives, and the senators of all fifty states owe their positions and power to the fact that they have run for election and been chosen by electoral majorities through a legitimate voting process.

Elections, to be legitimate, must be both free and fair. It follows that there are two types of voter suppression to guard against. The first is voter suppression that obstructs the ability of eligible voters to cast their ballots. Voter suppression of this type is obviously a subversion of democracy, has happened before in our history, and everyone is alert to it.

But we hear very little about the second type of voter suppression, though it, too, is a subversion of democracy and has also happened before. This is voter suppression that cancels out the votes of eligible voters through various forms of election fraud. In this case, not only do illegal votes cancel out legal votes, but if plentiful enough they can change the outcome of an election. A government elected by such a fictitious majority can rightly be called a junta or usurping power, because its power derives from corrupting free and fair elections.

The big question is whether the 2020 election was decided in this way, through a system of cheating large enough to alter the outcome. We're not talking about isolated instances of fraud—a dead man voting here, an illegal alien voting there—but rather about a criminal enterprise operating in key areas of the country to tip the presidential election and other key races to the Democrats.

The stakes could not be higher. We're asking whether the current occupant of the White House deserves to be there and whether the current distribution of power in the House and Senate is as it should be, or whether the process was corrupted through systematic election fraud. This book, building upon my documentary film investigating these questions, will provide new information and more detailed analysis to my answers.

•☞

What's new and startling about the 2020 election is not that a major party refused to accept the election results. This is the story we get from the Democrats and the media, but it's scarcely true. Joe Biden said of Trump, "He has done what no president in American history—the history of this country—has ever, ever done: He refused to accept the result of an election and the will of the American people."[2]

Yet Democrats have refused to accept election results for decades. The clearest example of this was, well, the previous election. The Democratic candidate, Hillary Clinton, subsequently said the election was stolen from her. Other leading Democrats, such as Jimmy Carter, have echoed this view.[3] A group of House Democrats objected to certifying the election results. Fully one-third of House Democrats refused to attend Donald Trump's inauguration, which was marred by leftist rioting.

Major figures in the Democratic Party and the media vowed they would not "normalize" Trump's presidency—and they kept that vow, calling themselves the "resistance" and defenders of a democracy in peril, routinely portraying Trump as a criminal, a racist, a white supremacist, and a Nazi.[4] Subsequently we learned that the Obama and Hillary teams promulgated a Russia collusion hoax to discredit Trump's election by falsely accusing him of reaching the presidency through treasonous collaboration with a foreign power.

For Democrats, election denial is something of a tradition. Democrats challenged the result of the Bush-Gore election in 2000, with many in Congress and in the media insisting Bush was "selected, not elected." Some Democrats disputed Bush's 2004 reelection win against

John Kerry, claiming that the voting machines in Ohio had been manipulated to deliver fraudulent votes to Bush. "In fact," writes Mollie Hemingway in her recent book *Rigged*, "the last time Democrats fully accepted the legitimacy of a presidential election they lost was in 1988."[5]

What's new is that, for the first time in recent history, many Republicans questioned the legitimacy of a presidential election. Republicans are the people who go along with election results, even when they lose. They might be sullen for a while, but they move on in the hope that they might win the next time. This is, in fact, what democratic politics should be. Losing an election should not be like losing a war.

But in 2020, losing an election was like losing a war. Why? Because a stolen election is something akin to a coup. It's one thing to lose fair and square, but something else entirely to be cheated of a victory that is rightfully yours. None of this seemed to perturb Mitch McConnell, the Republican leader in the Senate, who dismissed concerns about a stolen election and seemed to adjust just fine to having Joe Biden in the White House. McConnell even gave up his position as Senate majority leader with his usual equanimity, even though the result was produced by a strange and surreal runoff that gave Democrats two additional Senate seats in a clearly Republican state.

McConnell, however, was not typical of Republican voters. Despite McConnell's urging, a majority of voters from the party that normally shrugs its shoulders and moves on refused to move on from the 2020 election. In the aftermath of the election, a *Politico*–Morning Consult survey found that 64 percent of Republicans distrusted the result; more recent surveys show that number has only risen since then. "Nearly Three-Quarters of GOP Doubt Legitimacy of Biden's Win," read a December 2021 headline from *The Hill*.[6]

Republican distrust of the 2020 election result can be attributed to things that happened—things that Republican voters witnessed—before, during, and after the election.

Before: Republicans saw a decrepit Biden who barely campaigned, putting a "lid" on his schedule at noon or even earlier, while Trump energetically barnstormed across the country, drawing huge crowds at his rallies. When Biden held campaign events the media seemed to outnumber the attendees, and the mood was as flat and uninspiring as the candidate himself.

During: Republicans watched in dismay on Election Night as the counting of the votes was stopped for no apparent reason when Trump had a big lead in virtually all the key states, and then that lead mysteriously evaporated the next morning. I remember watching these events myself and thinking that, in more than forty years of living in America, I had never seen anything quite like this. I was also dumbfounded when Fox News called Arizona for Biden with a tiny percentage of the votes counted—no predictive calculus could have anticipated that Biden would eke out a victory that, as it turned out, was dependent on a few thousand votes. There were many other such "anomalies."

After: As Republicans pondered Biden's declared victory, they had to make sense of the fact that Trump had won the bellwether states of Ohio and Florida; he had won virtually all the bellwether counties that normally determine a presidential election; he had increased his vote total dramatically from 2016 (nearly 63 million votes) to more than 74 million votes—far better than Barack Obama had done in 2008 (fewer than 70 million votes) and 2012 (fewer than 66 million votes); and yet he had lost the election, because somehow Biden had increased the Democratic vote total even more dramatically, winning more than 80 million votes.

Consequently Republicans, after the 2020 election and the January 2021 Georgia runoffs, began to smell a rat. Many of them suspected—and some said openly, even stridently—that the 2020 election had been stolen. They made their voices heard on social media. They organized hearings and rallies, and they called for investigations and an adjudication of this issue. In voicing their distrust of the 2020 result they were merely echoing what Democrats had done, far more obstreperously and violently, in 2016. But Republicans, evidently, are not supposed to say such things. So this is when the trouble began.

⚏

Democrats responded to GOP protestations by insisting the 2020 election had been the most secure election in history. This was the uniform resounding cry from Democratic elected officials and the media. The same Democrats who had questioned the reliability of voting machines and the same media that had aired innumerable reports of the vulnerability of our election system to hacking and malfeasance now came together to affirm solemnly that this time around, the election had been impregnable. No problems whatsoever!

"Trump's Own Officials Say 2020 Was America's Most Secure Election in History." This headline in *Vox* reflects the Democratic party line. It appeals to a statement put out by the Department of Homeland Security's Cybersecurity and Infrastructure Security Agency (CISA). Chris Krebs, director of CISA, congratulated himself, saying, "We did a good job. I would do it one thousand times over." Such reassurances from credible officials, *Vox* said, contrasted with the "unfounded allegations of widespread voting irregularities and fraud" coming from Trump and other Republicans.[7]

Democrats did not, of course, deny that election fraud sometimes does occur. In October 2021 three women in separate counties in Michigan were charged with election fraud. One woman in Wayne

County signed and returned her grandson's ballot, claiming he would not have time to vote himself, but the grandson did end up voting in person, resulting in duplicate ballots being submitted. In Macomb County, a worker at an assisted living facility allegedly filled out ballot applications for assisted living residents and forged their signatures; she also used her own oversight to determine which residents should and should not receive absentee ballots. In another county a woman forged twenty-six absentee ballot applications on behalf of people under her guardianship and had their ballots sent to her, so she could vote on their behalf.

These cases are instructive—we will see later in this book how instructive—and we might expect that they would inspire broader investigations to determine the magnitude of this sort of fraud. Instead, Michigan secretary of state Jocelyn Benson said the charges prove "our election system is secure, and . . . demonstrate that in the rare circumstances when fraud occurs we catch it and hold the perpetrators responsible."[8] So cases of fraud are used here to repudiate the allegation of systematic fraud. See, only three fraudsters, and we got 'em!

In a similar—though slightly more sophisticated—gambit, the Associated Press (AP) reviewed what it claimed were all reported cases of voter fraud in six battleground states: Arizona, Georgia, Michigan, Nevada, Pennsylvania, and Wisconsin. Altogether, the AP found "fewer than 475 cases of potential voter fraud." Again, the AP's investigation into fraud was aimed not at finding fraud but at dismissing claims of widespread fraud.

"The cases could not throw the outcome into question even if all the potentially fraudulent votes were for Biden, which they were not, and even if those ballots were actually counted, which in most cases they were not." More than 80 percent of counties in these states, the AP said, had not even reported any suspicious activity.[9]

Once again, the message was clear: *Gee, Republicans, get over this stolen election nonsense. We've done the work for you, and there's nothing to see here.*

The problem with this project to vindicate the 2020 election is that it fails to convince even the moderately skeptical observer. In order to establish that the 2020 election was the most secure in history, wouldn't someone have to do a detailed comparison between the 2020 election and all previous elections in order to demonstrate that the volume of fraud in this election was markedly lower than in all the other elections? Not only has such a demonstration never been made; to my knowledge it has not even been attempted.

Is it really credible to ask the election officials themselves if this was the most secure election? What would you expect the very people running the election to say? Surely they will give the same answer you can expect if you ask a governor, "Hey, how well is your state being run?" or a district attorney, "How good an investigation did your office do in this case?"

Moreover, reported cases of fraud are typically rare, in the same manner that reported cases of drug use are rare, even though lots of Americans do in fact take drugs. Would it be reasonable to use such reported cases or cases of drug prosecutions to estimate the number of drug users in the country? I can envision a similar statement from the Michigan attorney general. "See, we've just caught three drug users, and this proves that we have zero tolerance for this practice and also that drug use is extremely rare in Michigan." Or an equally inane AP investigation aimed at showing that a mere 475 reported cases of drug use across six states confirms that there is no widespread problem of drug use in the country.

The tools used to carry out the investigation reported in this book—the investigation carried out by True the Vote—were all available to the various secretaries of state, not to mention to the Associated

Press. They all have the resources to purchase the data and the ability to gain access to the video evidence to determine for themselves the magnitude of election fraud. So why didn't they bother? The obvious reason is that they weren't looking for it. They didn't find it because they were determined not to find it. From the outset they were seeking to show not fraud, but the absence of fraud.

Democrats certainly did not want Republicans to seek or find election fraud, and they mobilized to prevent and block audits in the swing states. Indeed, they dismissed any discussion of election fraud in 2020 as a "big lie." The leftist tycoons who run social media—such figures as Jack Dorsey on Twitter and Mark Zuckerberg on Facebook—launched a massive campaign of censorship, banning and deplatforming hundreds of thousands, perhaps millions, of Americans for spreading what they termed election "misinformation" and "disinformation." Essentially, the topic of election fraud, although vividly present in many people's minds, was silenced.

In early 2022, the Biden Department of Justice classified Americans espousing "election lies" as potential domestic terrorists because their views could provoke others to violence, riots, and insurrection. Republican attempts to pass voter integrity laws to secure future elections were routinely portrayed by Democrats and their media allies as forms of "voter suppression." In effect, Democrats characterized the very mention of election fraud as a dangerous assault on the democratic process itself.

If Democratic assurances, crackdowns, and censorship were intended to produce Republican compliance and conformity, the result was quite the opposite. Republicans like my wife Debbie reasoned: "Why are they trying to shut us up about the election? If they have nothing to hide, if this was the most secure election, if they won cleanly and fairly, they should welcome our objections. They should themselves demand audits and court hearings. They should want to vindicate their electoral victory."

So naturally the Democratic vilification and bullying tactics intensified Republican anxieties. What made the whole situation so frustrating for Republicans, myself included, were the chaotic and confused attempts by some on the right to prove election fraud. They declared there was fraud; they insisted they had the proof; they said the proof was forthcoming; and yet they were unable to present it, not then when it counted, and not even after that. We were promised the release of the Kraken, but the Kraken never got released.

THE PILLOW GUY

A friend of mine, Mike Lindell, undertook, almost entirely on his own, a project to prove that election fraud had been committed through voting machines' altering votes. Lindell is a great guy, and his heart is in the right place. He is also immensely brave, and he suffered immediate cancellation and retaliation for even attempting to prove voter fraud. Dominion Voting Systems, which made the machines in question, filed a massive lawsuit against Lindell for maligning the integrity of the company. Lindell refused to back down, making a documentary called *Absolute Proof* and holding a cyber summit to publicize his claims.

I watched the documentary but, alas, I was left with a sinking feeling at the end. There was Lindell, excitedly pointing to various lights on the screen, declaring that the Chinese or various other foreign entities were hacking the U.S. election. I looked for Chinese, but didn't see any. I saw only lights on the screen. Naturally, as a film guy, I knew what I was seeing were mere "special effects." I know how to do that myself. This, to me, does not constitute proof of foreign powers hacking into our elections.

TRUMP

Moreover, I listened intently to the guys who made presentations at Lindell's cyber summit. I came away not so much confused as forced into a self-imposed "time out." It's very difficult to review the claims of those who claim cyber expertise—claims that will undoubtedly be disputed by other cyber experts—when we are not ourselves experts in this area. It's akin to ordinary people like you or me hearing various specialist doctors dispute about a diagnosis and then trying to figure out for ourselves who is right.

It's one thing to suspect that Trump won or that there was systematic fraud. It's one thing to point to oddities and anomalies that make it more likely that fraud could have occurred. It's also one thing to show how a breakdown of procedures made fraud more likely. Two excellent books, Mollie Hemingway's *Rigged* and *Our Broken Elections* by John Fund and Hans von Spakovsky, do exactly this. I would summarize those books as showing that the bank got rid of its security guards, turned off the surveillance system, and instructed the tellers not to do rigorous signature matching, all clearing the way for a bank heist. But the big question remains: Was there in fact a heist? On that question the two books are largely silent.

So it's one thing to allege fraud, and another thing to prove it. Democrats relished pointing out that the cases presented by the Trump campaign all went nowhere, and cases introduced by outside groups met the same fate. Texas, joined by several other red states, filed a claim to sue Democratic states for bending election rules. But the Supreme Court summarily dismissed the claim, curtly noting that Texas had no "standing" to sue. The Court took the position that the election conduct of some states is none of the other states' business, even though, as Texas pointed out, the tipping of those states had the effect of altering the result of a presidential election in a manner that affected the whole country.

I found the Supreme Court's blithe dismissal of the Texas case deeply troubling. But I also felt pretty certain that had the Supreme Court evaluated the claims of fraud and malfeasance, as I think it should have, it would have upheld the election results. Even if Texas and the other plaintiff states could show procedural violations and election irregularities, they could not, in my view, demonstrate that these had been sufficient to tip the election. A Supreme Court review would have gone far to allay public concerns—it might even have prevented the January 6, 2021, incursion into the Capitol—but substantively, I believe, it would leave us with the same result we have now.

For my own part, I eagerly awaited, through the weeks and months following the election, some convincing demonstration of election fraud. None came. Consequently, I have been largely silent on the topic. To quote my Salem Media colleague Dennis Prager, who took the same position, I have been an "agnostic" on the issue. Yes, the whole thing was a strange business. Yes, none of it made sense.

But if the Democrats stole Fort Knox, they had evidently committed the perfect crime. Indeed, legally they had gotten away with it. In the words of Salem's chairman, Ed Atsinger, "If they stole the election, they stole it fair and square." Atsinger's point is that the Republicans should have known this was coming. Trump predicted it, after all. The Republican National Committee raised money to investigate and bust election fraud. So why wasn't there a plan in place to catch the thieves in the act, or at least expose them afterward and bring them to justice? Basically, Atsinger feels the GOP is partly to blame because if there was a heist, we let them pull it off undetected.

The reason we need proof is because it's not obvious that Trump won the 2020 election. It's quite possible, in other words, that he lost. I realize there are many Republicans who think this is preposterous, but I am not one of them. After all, Covid decimated the Trump economy so that the gains Trump spelled out in his 2020 State of the Union were all gone by election time. Covid, Jane Fonda said, was "God's gift to the Left," and this is one sense in which that was certainly true.

Trump also performed very badly in the first debate. Debbie and I watched that debate, and we had the dismaying sense that he was throwing away his chances for reelection. We could just envision suburbanites across the country shaking their heads and saying, "Enough of this. We're done with this guy!" So while Trump made inroads among the working class, including the black and Hispanic working class, it's conceivable he lost just as many, if not more, suburban voters, and the margin was sufficient to cost him the election.

Whatever the truth about election fraud in the 2020 election, over time the case seemed to go cold. Leading Republicans took the position that it was time to pack up and move on. In early 2022, Senator Mike Rounds proclaimed that "the election was fair, as fair as we have seen. We simply did not win the election." Senator Kevin Cramer said, "The election was not stolen—at least to the degree that it was illegal theft." He added, "I've moved on a long time ago, and most members of Congress have." Senators Lindsey Graham and Mitch McConnell have conveyed the same sentiments.[10] This is the familiar Republican "grin and bear it" strategy. It suggests not so much an intellectual position—there was no systematic fraud—as a psychological one—we are in no mood to fight.

But there is a very high cost to swallowing our doubts and moving on. Republicans are grimly aware that if the Democrats cheated in the 2020 presidential election and in the Georgia U.S. Senate runoffs in 2021, they are likely to think they can cheat again in 2022, 2024, and every election beyond that. These were my fears, these were my despondent reflections, when Debbie and I were approached by two of Debbie's old friends, Catherine Engelbrecht and Gregg Phillips. They had a story that needed to be told, and they wanted our help telling it. The spent the better part of a day showing us extraordinary evidence, and by the end of that fateful day, I knew that the game had changed and that we could finally resolve the issue of what happened in the 2020 election.

CHAPTER 2

True the Vote

Election fraud is hard to catch, even when it's going on in plain sight. In May 2021, a man was captured on video stuffing multiple ballots in a drop box in Lackawanna County, Pennsylvania, during a primary election. Lackawanna County commissioner Chris Chermak obtained the security footage through a public information request and shared it during a board meeting. Yet the sheriff of the county said he had neither the time nor the manpower to review the video or act on its evidence.

Moreover, Chermak said that Democrats on the board, while agreeing the video showed improper conduct, refused to concede that the votes deposited in the drop box were fraudulent or mattered to the total number of ballots. Under Pennsylvania law, a voter can return only his own completed ballot unless he has written permission to submit one on behalf of a disabled person. Otherwise, possessing other people's ballots is a crime, and conviction can carry a 2-year prison sentence and a $5,000 fine.[1]

In the lead-up to the 2020 election, the Trump campaign was notified that three people had been observed illegally dropping off multiple ballots into an unmanned drop box. The campaign called on election officials to take action and man the drop boxes. Election officials didn't do anything except notify the *New York Times*, which accused Trump campaign observers of engaging in "voter intimidation."[2]

The *Philadelphia Inquirer* published a similar story, quoting Democratic attorney general Josh Shapiro to the effect that observing ballot box election fraud constituted voter intimidation. The story was illustrated with a photograph captioned: "Philadelphia Mayor Jim Kenney delivers his mail ballot outside City Hall on Monday." The Democratic mayor was actually shown with *two* ballots, a clear violation of state law.[3]

Asked about this, the mayor's office admitted he had been seen with two ballots, but insisted he had been rescued at the last minute from breaking the law. "The mayor was also carrying a mail-in ballot belonging to a person with whom he is personally close," Kenney spokesman Mike Dunn said. "The elections official standing with him in the photograph informed him that he was not allowed to deposit that person's ballot. The mayor then deposited only his own ballot into the drop box."[4]

In 2020, before the election, James O'Keefe's undercover reporters of Project Veritas embedded themselves within the Somali community in Congresswoman Ilhan Omar's district in Minnesota, and they found sources who told them exactly how illegal ballot harvesting worked in the district, with teams going door to door with absentee ballot forms and essentially buying votes.

Project Veritas identified a Somali vote trafficker named Liban Mohamed who boasted of having hundreds of absentee ballots in his car. "Numbers don't lie. You can see my car is full. All these here are absentee ballots. Can't you see. Look at all these. My car is full." Mohamed took videos of himself recording his unlawful conduct. One of them showed him flipping through a stack of ballots, wielding them like playing cards while singing about his accomplishments.[5]

What was the reaction? Several journalists insisted that ballot harvesting is legal in Minnesota. But Minnesota law says that no one can deliver more than three ballots belonging to someone else to a drop box. This law was challenged in court and its enforcement temporarily stayed, but the law itself remained in effect and was then upheld by the Minnesota Supreme Court. Yet no action was taken to hold the ballot harvesters accountable.

The *New York Times* published several hit pieces on the Project Veritas report, calling it "deceptive," "disinformation," and "false." When Project Veritas sued the *Times* for defamation, the newspaper took the revealing position that its reporters were not transmitting facts but rather opinions. The *Times* basically admitted that its reporters do not distinguish opinion from fact, and had not factually contradicted Project Veritas's reporting.[6]

Both in the Pennsylvania and Minnesota cases, no action was taken against alleged perpetrators of election fraud for two reasons. One, the media helped cover up these violations, and two, the responsibility to take action fell on Democratic officials committed to the narrative that elections are largely foolproof and voter fraud is rare and inconsequential.

Granted, these examples show episodic rather than systematic violations. Nevertheless, they are suggestive and highlight the pressing need for an experienced, sophisticated, resourceful, courageous, and persistent group to investigate systematic election fraud, knowing full well that it would face legal attacks, media dismissals, and social media censorship. In Texas, there was such a group.

When Catherine Engelbrecht called my wife Debbie to propose a meeting, the topic of election fraud was entirely taboo, the sort of thing that might get my podcast banned from Facebook, YouTube, and possibly Twitter. Consequently, there was no discussion of election fraud in the public domain. It was discussed on Steve Bannon's *War Room* and in a few other precincts, but, in general, the digital tycoons—egged on by the Biden administration and the Democrats—had successfully silenced postmortem debate about what had happened in the 2020 election.

"Catherine says they have something new," Debbie said. "They" referred to Catherine and her business partner, Gregg Phillips. Debbie had been friends with Catherine for many years. In fact, Catherine's nonprofit group True the Vote had trained Debbie as a poll watcher in Fort Bend County, Texas. Debbie had served both as a poll watcher and a poll worker in various elections going back to 2012, and she had observed clear cases of election malfeasance firsthand.

In one case, Debbie saw a Hispanic poll judge instruct voters not only about how to vote but for whom they should vote. Debbie speaks Spanish, and when she confronted the poll judge, the judge quickly stopped her illegal coaching of voters. Yet Debbie was at the polling place for only a couple of days of early voting. Who knows if the poll judge returned to her old ways when Debbie was gone? Catherine told Debbie that voter coaching is a big problem in polling places around the country.

Catherine Engelbrecht founded True the Vote in 2010 as a nonprofit organization to get citizens involved in the process of ensuring honest elections. She's a tall, striking, somewhat shy and yet passionate woman. In the words of a *Texas Observer* profile, "Her blond hair and aviator sunglasses gave her the air of an aging Hollywood bombshell." She was a mom and local businesswoman when she volunteered to work the polls in Texas. What she saw convinced her of the need for an organization that would monitor and help to expose election fraud. Inspired by the Tea Party movement, Catherine also founded a group called King Street Patriots.

Almost immediately after setting up these two organizations—King Street Patriots and True the Vote—Catherine came under the scrutiny of the Obama administration. In fact, this is what propelled her into the national limelight. She testified to Congress in 2014 about how she, her family, her private manufacturing business, and her nonprofit organizations had been targeted by multiple federal organizations.

Catherine testified (and her testimony is available online, if you want to watch) that in 2011 her "personal and business tax returns were audited by the Internal Revenue Service, each audit going back for a number of years." The IRS, according to Catherine, "subjected me to multiple rounds of abusive inquiries, with requests to provide every Facebook and Twitter entry I'd ever posted, questions about my political aspirations, and demands to know the names of every group I'd ever made presentations to, the content of what I'd said, and where I intended to speak for the coming year."

Catherine continued, "In 2012, my business was subjected to inspection by OSHA. . . . In 2012 and again in 2013 the Bureau of Alcohol, Tobacco and Firearms conducted comprehensive audits at my place of business. Beginning in 2012, the FBI contacted my nonprofit organization on six separate occasions, wanting to cull through membership manifests." All of this started when she created a voter integrity group. "There is no other remarkable event, no other reason, to explain how for decades I went unnoticed, but now find myself on the receiving end of interagency coordination into and against all facets of my life, both public and private."

I met Catherine and her business partner, Gregg Phillips, through Debbie. Phillips for his part is a handsome, bearded guy with a deep voice. In the 1990s he served as head of the Mississippi Department of Human Services, and in the early 2000s he was deputy commissioner for the Texas Health and Human Services Commission. Now he works with Catherine on the issue of election fraud, a topic he's investigated for decades.

Catherine has been sued more times than she can remember, by the Texas Democratic Party, by a left-wing group called Texans for Public Justice, most recently by Stacey Abrams's group Fair Fight. The latest skirmish involves True the Vote's challenge to more than 300,000 names on the voter rolls in Georgia—names that Catherine suspects are people who have died, people who have moved, or people who are for some other reason ineligible to vote.

For reasons that will become clear later, groups like Fair Fight are desperate to keep the voter rolls as they are—full of inaccurate or obsolete data—because they believe it serves their interests. "Sorry, guys," Catherine said on one of our recent calls, "I just finished my day-long deposition with Fair Fight. Twelve hours! It was grueling. These people are ruthless. They have unlimited resources, and they will stop at nothing. They are determined to block the work we are doing."

In both the weeks ahead of the 2020 election and in the immediate aftermath, there was a frenzy of activity in which the Trump campaign, Rudy Giuliani, the attorney Sidney Powell, Mike Lindell, and many others raised multiple questions about election fraud. During this period, Debbie and I noticed that Catherine was completely silent. We found this odd. Here was this huge outcry over voter fraud, and the leading organization that had monitored this issue for more than a decade had nothing to say about it.

I called Catherine, and she warned me to stay away from some of the wilder accusations. "A lot of this stuff is completely crazy," she said. "I'm afraid it's making our whole side look irresponsible. And it's making it more difficult to make legitimate arguments, because they get mixed in with the rest."

Catherine added, "I'm not saying everyone else is wrong. I am saying they will never be able to prove what they are saying. As a practical matter, they're going up a blind alley." Debbie and I asked Catherine what we could do to help. It would help most, she said, if we would make a video calling on whistleblowers to come forward and contact True the Vote with information they might have on election fraud.

And so we did, as did many of Catherine's other friends with a social media presence. Little did we know at that time how important this call to action would prove. Still, based on Catherine's counsel, I refrained from commenting in public on voter fraud and claims of machines switching votes, Chinese hacking, and the rest, even though this didn't make my friend Mike Lindell very happy. I avoided the topic for more than a year—until we met with Catherine and Gregg at our home in Texas.

"We have something new to show you." Catherine and Gregg's presentation of their evidence lasted several hours. We asked questions along the way. When they were finished, Catherine said, "Our work is ongoing, but that's what we have so far. What do you think?" I was impressed, to say the least.

We talked about money. True the Vote's investigation into the 2020 election was made possible by an unsolicited donation from Fred Eshelman, a billionaire entrepreneur and Republican donor who approached True the Vote through consultants. He promised a $2.5 million gift to support the group's work on election fraud.

And that's when the trouble started.

As Catherine tells the story, just days after she received the funds, Eshelman's consultants submitted a bill for $1 million. She stared at the invoice, dumbfounded. In effect, Eshelman's team had given them $2.5 million and now wanted nearly half the money back. Catherine said she worried that this was some sort of "kickback," that the donors were giving tax-deductible funds to a nonprofit and then retrieving it for other purposes.

True the Vote's lawyer, Jim Bopp, instructed Catherine that it would be highly problematic and most likely illegal for her to make a payback of this magnitude. Eshelman's side of the story was that he had made a "conditional gift," based on assurances that True the Vote would file a series of court cases making election fraud claims. Since those cases were never filed, Eshelman said he had a right to get his money back.

Catherine told us that Eshelman's gift was not conditional, that there were no documents that specified any conditions, and that True the Vote had prepared legal filings based on "equal protection" claims but had not filed them, in large part because courts showed little interest in adjudicating the issue. Rather than racing to accumulate and assess evidence before Biden's inauguration—an effort that was doomed to failure—True the Vote decided to focus its inquiries in a different way.

The organization communicated this to Eshelman's team, but negotiations between the parties broke down. Eshelman sued in federal court, then withdrew the case, refiled it in state court, and that suit was dismissed. "The whole thing was an ordeal," Catherine told us. "But at least it's over. And at least it gave us the resources to launch this project, although a chunk of it got eaten up in legal fees."

Catherine and Gregg said they wanted to share their initial findings with us because they trusted us to advise them on the best way to tell their story. They had several ideas. Breitbart, Gateway Pundit, and other conservative online outlets were very interested in their work. A persistent journalist, John Solomon, wanted the scoop. Tucker Carlson wanted to have Catherine on for a big news hit. Other TV outlets like One America News and Newsmax might also be receptive.

I told Catherine and Gregg that in my opinion it would be a mistake to release their findings piecemeal. The reason was that the Left was highly mobilized on this issue. They would swat down each claim with their inevitable rants about "conspiracy theories" and "here we go again." Even with a highly visible interview with Tucker Carlson, the story would be a one-day sensation. I recommended that we consider doing a full-length documentary film based on, and building upon, the research of True the Vote.

My argument was that a movie is a uniquely powerful way to deliver the sort of explosive content that True the Vote had discovered in its ongoing investigation. "Let's put the facts and the story together in one piece," I suggested, "and let the American people be the judge."

Catherine and Gregg agreed, but the decision to go in this direction wasn't up to me alone. At that time, I had already contracted with Salem Media—sponsors of my podcast—to do a film on free speech and censorship. "Silenced" was our working title. Salem had put up $1.5 million in equity for my company, D'Souza Media, to produce and make the movie. We intended to market it through another $3 million in loans. This is, roughly, the formula that I have used with my previous movies, although typically I have a group of investors and the numbers are considerably higher: $5 million or so in equity, another $5 million in marketing loans.

Recognizing the sensitivity of the topic of election fraud, I proposed organizing a summit with the top leadership at Salem, including the chairman and head honcho, Ed Atsinger, to see if we could get the whole team on board with this new topic. At first, the Salem team was very skeptical—and nervous too, because they recognized this topic was out of bounds—but they agreed to meet with me and Catherine and Gregg and hear us out.

Catherine and Gregg gave their presentation, and there were questions galore. The questions, initially dismissive and hostile, then respectful and curious, in the end became admiring and incredulous: "How on earth have you two managed to do what no one else has?" We came to a unanimous decision that we had no alternative but to take up this topic, with all its risks—media derision, social media censorship, litigation, even danger to our personal security—and go ahead.

There was, however, another problem. I had urged True the Vote to remain silent so that we could tell the full story in a film—a film that was several months away from being finished. How, then, could Catherine and Gregg raise the money they needed to continue and complete their investigation? There was only one solution: Debbie and I had to help.

We called up two of our friends—one in Jacksonville, Florida, and another in Wichita, Kansas—who agreed to meet with Catherine. The consequence was that our two friends gave $400,000 between them, and True the Vote was able to push forward and complete its investigation.

When I first visited the Grand Canyon, as an eighteen-year-old, I learned that there are two ways down to the bottom. The first, of course, is to walk. The second is to ride a mule. I was with a group of fellow exchange students from around the world, and we chose to hike our way down. But along the way I saw mules slowly and sure-footedly carrying passengers down some very steep paths.

Here we're going to talk about a very different type of mule—a paid vote trafficker. Catherine and Gregg came up with the term, which they borrowed from the "mules" involved in drug and human trafficking. "It seemed appropriate to us," Catherine said, "because vote trafficking works in pretty much the same way." In the drug trade, the mule is the guy who brings the drugs across the border into America. In sex trafficking, the mule is the go-between who connects the captive women with the men who buy, use, and exploit them.

In the domain of election fraud, the mule is the paid operative who delivers the illegal ballots to ballot drop boxes. It should be noted that while voter harvesting is legal in some states—for instance, in California it is legal to have someone drop your ballot off for you—in no state is it legal to have *paid operatives* deliver ballot applications or ballots themselves. So an operation involving mules is prima facie illegal, and the ballots delivered by the mules are all illegal ballots. This is election fraud, pure and simple.

We caught a break when David Lara of San Luis, Arizona, stepped forward as a whistleblower. He had heard about True the Vote, and he called its hotline. In Arizona, "San Luis is ground zero as far as voter fraud," Lara said. "That's where it started in 1997. It has spread through the state, and it was perfected in San Luis."

Lara and his friend and fellow businessman Gary Garcia Snyder suspected rampant voting fraud in San Luis, but they needed proof. On August 4, 2020, election primary day, Snyder arrived at 7:00 a.m. at one of San Luis's two polling stations. Lara left to observe the other polling site. "I pop in my iPad and put Netflix on," Snyder said, "so that they think I'm just watching Netflix, but during that whole time I was recording any movement, any voters that would walk up to their booths. And yep, within 5 to 10 minutes after David left, the first crime was committed."

Snyder recorded several videos, one of which shows Guillermina Fuentes, a member of the Gadsden Elementary School District board, receiving multiple ballots from a woman named Alma Yadira Juarez. Based on the video evidence—which Lara turned in to Yuma County recorder Robyn Pouquette—the sheriff was notified, and he in turn notified the attorney general's office and the FBI. Both women were indicted for felony ballot abuse. Alma Yadira Juarez turned state's evidence against Guillermina Fuentes, who pleaded guilty in the immediate aftermath of the release of the documentary *2000 Mules*.

Lara says that election fraud is a way of life in the Latino and low-income neighborhoods of Yuma County. Mules who work for political bosses pay people to hand over their blank mail-in ballots along with the signed ballot affidavit envelope. Note that mail-in ballots themselves are not signed, but eligible voters are required to sign the outer envelope testifying that they are the ones who have cast the ballot.

Except in these cases, they haven't. Rather, they give their ballots to the mules, who turn them over to the political organizers, and the political organizers then fill in the ballots, marking them for the candidates of their choice. They place the ballots in the signed envelopes, seal them, and have the mules drop off the ballots, which are fraudulent ballots but are nevertheless counted as valid votes.

"It's done in such a manner that . . . the community believes it's the norm," Lara says. "They think it's acceptable and they think this is the way it's done." The voters, in other words, are not even aware they are committing fraud, which is why, in these contexts, the term "voter fraud" is not appropriate. The correct term is "election fraud." Why? Because that's what the political bosses and their mules are after. They want to fraudulently fix the outcome of elections.

Lara describes how it works. "So what happens is this: You go to a nonprofit as a member of the community, and you ask for help. It could be housing, it could be health, it could be whatever, filling out documents, you name it. When you walk in, they will ask you, oh, by the way, are you registered to vote? Oh, well, no, I'm not. Is your family registered? No. Well, we can help you."

What the nonprofit activists do is build trust with the new voter, who is likely to seek assistance in understanding the ballot. At this point, Lara says, the voter is told, "Well, don't worry about it, just sign it and I'll take care of it for you." Alternatively, they are told whom to vote for.

Lara says election fraud is part of the way that the local Democratic establishment perpetuates its power. "Being a board member, and especially if you have the majority, if your party or your group has a majority on the school board, then you control each year the hires, new hires, rehires, contracts, fires. So what happens is if somebody wants a job—bring me your ballots, your neighbor's ballots, your family's. It becomes a web."

Election fraud, in other words, is a form of compliance to get by in San Luis. Lara says, "They've actually tricked the community into believing they're doing the right thing, they're voting, they're participating, yet they're not really informing the community that they're being lied to, used, and manipulated."[7]

•━

We caught another break when one of the mules agreed to talk. She cooperated with the authorities and resolved her case. Even so, she wouldn't talk to me on camera with our film crew present. But she did agree to be interviewed by Gregg Phillips. Gregg filmed the interview in such a manner that her face and identity were concealed; that's how we were able to use excerpts of the interview in the movie. But of course we only used a small part of the conversation in the film, so I'm offering a longer portion here. While I've edited the interview for length, what's here is verbatim, coming from the mouth of the mule herself.

Gregg: So when this whole adventure started, what were you doing?

Mule: I was working for a construction company.

Gregg: What was your job?

Mule: Receptionist.

Gregg: So at some point, you were asked or sort of instructed, I guess, to start receiving people's ballots.

Mule: Correct. I was just instructed to go ahead and receive ballots from various people. Females mostly. And on Friday they would come and pick up payment, I assume it was payment, for what they were doing.

Gregg: So they would during the week bring them in at various times and then you would pay them, like all on a Friday? Is that how it went?

Mule: Yes.

Gregg: Did you know any of these people?

Mule: I didn't personally know them, but they're very known in the city of San Luis.

Gregg: Why do you think they were participating? What was in it for them?

Mule: I would say it was money. They would bring them into the office and drop them off. And then I would get a call to find out how many were brought in.

Gregg: So during the early election time when people were getting these ballots at their homes—and the collectors or harvesters would come to pick them up, would you get multiple drop-offs during the day?

Mule: It was like every once in a while during the week. But it would be significant sometimes amounts of them.

Gregg: Do you have any idea how many would come in during an election?

Mule: Not necessarily but it was quite some. And in particular, one of them, I did speak to her because she was my neighbor. She lived four houses away from me. And I told her, why was she bringing it? She said she'd been doing it for many years already.

Gregg: Do you have any idea how much people were getting paid for these ballots?

Mule: Not necessarily, because the envelopes, we would always leave them closed. But it was cash. I know it wasn't a check because you can tell when it's cash.

Gregg: And then sometimes you said she asked you to go to the library. What was the instruction?

Mule: Just to drop them off.

Gregg: In the drop box?

Mule: Uh, huh. The drop box. The early ballots.

Gregg: Can you give me an idea of how many you personally put in the box? Hundreds?

Mule: Could have been, yes.

Gregg: And was there a reason she wanted you to go to that drop box as opposed to maybe city hall?

Mule: There's no cameras there. And she would want me to take it in the evening when it was dark also.

Gregg: So in your view—maybe you don't know the answer to this—but how long does this seem like something they've been doing?

Mule: Forever.

Gregg: Why do you think the ballot harvesters themselves did it?

Mule: For the money, I think.

Gregg: And why do you think she did it?

Mule: I think she was getting paid too—I wouldn't doubt it. Because she wouldn't risk anything like that, getting in trouble for nothing. There's got to be something behind it. Other than just wanting to beat the opponents.

Gregg: You think this is widespread in Yuma County or elsewhere?

Mule: I would say it is.

Gregg: Do you think that people you know in San Luis believe that their vote matters?

Mule: I don't even think they know the meaning of what voting is, most of them. . . . Most of the Hispanics that live in the town are not well educated as far as the law. They think that, oh if she is offering this, they look at it mostly as, oh she's trying to help us. . . . And when I first moved into the city of San Luis, I did have somebody come and knock on my door and ask for my ballot. And it was somebody I knew, and that I had known for many years since I was a child. And up to this day, this person does not talk to me because I said there was no way I was giving them my ballot.

Gregg: Do you think it's about—what is this? Is it party? What is it?

Mule: I call it the Mexican Mafia. Seriously. Because they work like that. Living in San Luis, it's like living in Mexico—just the only difference, it's not across the border.

Gregg: Do you personally think the elections in San Luis are free and fair?

Mule: No. They're fixed. They've been fixed. They already know, seriously, who is going to win the next election before it even happens.

Gregg: It seems like we need to do a better job of maybe educating folks—or helping people understand—that this stuff is not okay.

Mule: Yes. And I offered. A long time ago. But again, they told me, oh don't do it. Because you're going to end up in a trash can, in pieces. Because they have that much power.

Gregg: Are you scared?

Mule: My mom used to say when I was little, that the devil would be scared of [me] instead of me of the devil. I'm not afraid of anything, to be honest.

Gregg: What do you think it's going to take to get this trafficking to stop?

Mule: For people to get caught. To get caught and pay the price.

CHAPTER 3

What Is Geotracking?

There are many different types of election fraud. True the Vote has published an election integrity guide, and it lists seven types of illegal interference in the process of an election.

1. *False registrations*: Using bogus or phony names and addresses or claiming residency where the voters do not live and are not eligible to vote
2. *Impersonation fraud at the polls*: Voting in the name of legitimate voters, or in the name of voters who have moved or died but not been removed from the voter rolls
3. *Illegal "assistance" or intimidation*: Guiding elderly or vulnerable persons by telling them whom to vote for or coercing or pressuring them to vote for a given candidate or party
4. *Ineligible voting* by non-citizens, felons, and others not eligible to vote

5. *Duplicate voting* in the same election in more than one state or jurisdiction

6. *Fraudulent use of absentee or mail-in ballots* obtained with or without voters' knowledge, forging their ballots or coercing them to vote a particular way

7. *Buying or selling votes*[1]

Does election fraud occur? It's hard to detect and prove, so the full extent of election fraud is not known. What is known is that there have been innumerable documented and proven cases of election fraud. True the Vote has an online database that includes a sampling of cases from around the country. This database documents hundreds of fraud convictions as well as numerous elections that were overturned due to proven fraud.

The Heritage Foundation also maintains an Election Fraud Database. It includes, when I last checked, 1,340 instances of fraud and 1,152 criminal convictions, along with numerous other official findings, judicial findings, and civil penalties. These are not a compilation of media reports or mere allegations of fraud. They represent cases where fraud is proven or established in a federal, state, or local election.

"Each and every one of the cases in this database represents an instance in which a public official, usually a prosecutor, thought the fraud serious enough to act upon it. And each and every one ended in a finding that the individual had engaged in wrongdoing in connection with an election hoping to affect its outcome—or that the results of an election were altered or sufficiently in question and had to be overturned."[2]

Interestingly in late 2020, *USA Today*, PBS *Frontline*, and Columbia Journalism Investigations dispatched a whole team of reporters to investigate the Heritage database and try to find errors that could then be used to discredit the perception of pervasive election fraud. The team found no errors, so they resorted to citing left-wing academics to the effect that in most cases election fraud is not widespread enough to change the outcome of elections. We see here a pattern that persists to this day—the media is not genuinely interested in substantiating election fraud, only in disproving it in order to affirm the result of the 2020 presidential election.

These media denials notwithstanding, election fraud has been a staple feature of American democracy. The Supreme Court in 2008, while upholding Indiana's new voter ID law, recognized a long history of election fraud in the United States. "Flagrant examples of such fraud," the Court said, "have been documented throughout this nation's history," demonstrating that "not only is the risk of voter fraud real but that it could affect the outcome of a close election." These words were written by John Paul Stevens, arguably the most liberal justice on the Court at the time.[3]

The party of voter fraud in America is—I expect this will not come as a big surprise—the Democratic Party. In my book *Hillary's America*, which is subtitled *The Secret History of the Democratic Party*, I show how the founder of the Democratic Party, Andrew Jackson, essentially bought the votes of white settlers by promising them land obtained by forcibly driving Native Americans off their ancestral territories.

Tammany Hall, and the system of party bosses that came to dominate major cities in the second half of the nineteenth century, became a symbol of Democratic corruption. Not all the bosses were Democrats—Philadelphia, for example, had a Republican boss who was just as unscrupulous as any Democrat—but most of them were, and they did not hesitate to create patronage systems in which they provided jobs, housing, and all kinds of benefits in exchange for votes. In some cases, the Tammany fraudsters would simply give people pre-marked ballots and observe as they dropped them into the voting box.[4]

In *Our Broken Elections*, John Fund and Hans von Spakovsky describe an 1864 ballot fraud scheme organized by the New York Democrats. Mail-in ballots had been legalized for Union troops, and in a bid to prevent the reelection of Abraham Lincoln, a ballot trafficker named Moses Ferry, an ally of New York's Democratic governor Horatio Seymour, created an elaborate scheme to collect mail-in ballots from military regiments and sick and wounded troops in hospitals and used them to deliver fraudulent votes for the Democratic presidential candidate, George McClellan.[5]

The Democrats, of course, were notorious for election fraud and voter suppression in the Jim Crow era, in which the Ku Klux Klan—which operated as the military wing of the Democratic Party—used racial terrorism to suppress not only blacks but also white Republicans from going to the polls. Robert Caro and others have recounted how Lyndon Johnson stole his first Senate election in Texas in 1948. And while there is still some dispute about this, it also appears that election fraud in Texas and in Cook County, Illinois, delivered the presidency to Democrat John F. Kennedy over his Republican opponent Richard Nixon in 1960.[6]

This is not to say that all election fraud is perpetrated by the Democrats. Occasionally we do find cases of Republicans indulging in such corruption. In their 2021 book *The Vote Collectors*, Michael Graff and Nick Ochsner tell how a crafty character named McCrae Dowless illegally trafficked absentee ballots for Republican congressional candidate Mark Harris in Bladen County, North Carolina, in 2018.

I'll describe later how Dowless pulled it off, but his fraud was so egregious that the election result was overturned. Mark Harris, the Republican who had narrowly "won" the election against Democrat Dan McCready, acknowledged his victory was suspect, called for a new election, and pulled out of the race. (The Republicans nominated a new candidate, Dan Bishop, who went on to beat McCready in the 2019 special election.) The point I want to make here, though, is that Dowless was a Republican fraudster.

Even here, however, the story has a twist. Dowless learned how to do illegal vote trafficking from the Democrats. Dowless used to work for a left-wing Democratic PAC called the Bladen County Improvement Association. This African American activist group specialized in "getting out the vote," interpreting the term loosely as forging ballot applications, casting votes on behalf of others, using paid traffickers, showing up to vote at more than one location, and numerous other shenanigans that made Dowless a sort of specialist in election fraud.

A bitter feud with the Democrats, however, provoked Dowless to break with his old allies and offer his paid services to the Republican candidate, who didn't know about Dowless's true expertise in election fraud but had heard that he was a guy who knew how to get votes.[7] Interestingly, when *The Vote Collectors* was published the media trumpeted it because it pointed to Republican fraud, and Republicans, too, seized upon it because it confirmed that election fraud, and specifically absentee ballot fraud, is real.

So yes, election fraud is real and yes, the bad guys are usually Democrats. But was fraud an important factor in the most recent presidential election? How much fraud? Who did the fraud? And of the varied types of fraud to choose from, what type of fraud did they use? Finally, how to prove it? These were the questions that vexed Catherine Engelbrecht as she surveyed the turbulent landscape of the 2020 election.

◆

Catherine took her first cue from the whistleblower in Arizona and the mule operation he described—an operation that was subsequently recognized by the Arizona district attorney and resulted in indictments, prosecutions, and plea deals. That's how we got our mule to talk—she cooperated and was legally immunized, although she still has good reason to worry about her security. What she described, however, was a whole operation, virtually a way of life, directed by the Democrats who control the area and involving the fraudulent trafficking of absentee and mail-in ballots. Could it be, Catherine wondered, that this operation was not local to Yuma or even Arizona but operated nationwide?

Fraud, in the experience of Catherine and True the Vote, is typically an old-school operation. Fraudsters prefer not to have to reinvent the wheel. If there's a tried-and-true racket that's worked for them before, why not go with it again? This is not an argument against new possibilities, such as manipulated machines and so on, but it is to say that Democrats have developed fraud techniques over the decades, and it just so happens that these old-school ways are now greatly facilitated by the new environment created by Covid-19.

Absentee ballot fraud has been widely recognized by students of elections to be the easiest and most common form of fraud. This is precisely what a bipartisan election commission co-chaired by Jimmy Carter stated in 2005. And why is that the case? Because absentee voting is the only type of voting that takes place away from the normal, secure environment of a voting booth. Voting booths enforce privacy for the voter; absentee votes have none of that. There is no easy way in a voting place to pressure or intimidate voters, fill out their ballots and cast their votes for them, or pay them to vote one way or another, but all of this becomes possible when the voter is outside the monitored area.

Mail-in ballots were permitted and used in a number of places before the 2020 presidential election, but their use became much more widespread and normalized during this election. Suddenly, the Covid pandemic gave Democrats a way to make mail-in voting even more common. Only a quarter of all voters used a mail-in ballot during the 2016 and 2018 elections, but that number rose to more than 43 percent in 2020; and of the remaining voters, about half voted early in person, and the other half showed up to vote on Election Day.[8]

Thus, Catherine reasoned, if Democrats were going to expand their fraud operations in 2020, they would do it here, using drop boxes and mail-in ballots to carry out coordinated vote trafficking. Catherine knew that in Arizona the traffickers used various commercial and nonprofit "stash houses" as venues where the fraudulent ballots would be assembled, and then mules like the one we interviewed would be recruited to make drop-offs, typically nocturnal drop-offs, to ballot drop boxes where the bad ballots would then be mixed in with other legitimate ones.

This led Catherine and Gregg Phillips to formulate a hypothesis and devise an ingenious way to test it. The hypothesis was that the Democrats and their allies were committed to getting rid of Trump "by any means necessary." They regarded Trump as virtually a fascist and a Nazi, so why not? The ends justify the means, and if it has to be election fraud, so be it. The main thing is to make it work, to get away with the heist. The mechanism for carrying out the heist was an assortment of leftist nonprofit centers, which would serve as the stash houses.

The nonprofits would be charged with coming up with the fraudulent votes. (How they do this is the subject of a later chapter.) The mules would be paid to deliver the votes. Note that the use of paid mules automatically renders every vote they deliver fraudulent and illicit. In no state is it permissible to hire paid operatives to deliver votes, but when you're delivering enough fraudulent votes to tip a national election, you likely need paid operatives. Continuing with Catherine and Gregg's hypothesis, unsupervised ballot drop boxes would be the targets where mules could deliver the fraudulent votes.

Now this, Catherine and Gregg recognized, is merely a hypothesis, a theory. There is very little value in a theory, even a plausible one, if it cannot be tested. The real genius of True the Vote is that it developed a foolproof system to test the theory. The system, which uses new technology to investigate an old-school fraud scheme, goes by the name of geotracking. True the Vote would use geotracking to figure out if there was fraud in the swing states, and how much, and who did it, and which organizations were behind it. "If they did it this way," Catherine told Debbie and me, "we have a reliable way to bust them."

Geotracking is the system of identifying the current or past physical location of individuals by obtaining data from their cellphones. Our cellphones contain within them apps that store information—weather apps, news apps, even retail apps—and this information is connected to our specific cellphone IDs that reveal our precise location at any given moment. Data companies such as Foursquare collect this information, and some of them sell it or make it available for commercial, intelligence-gathering, or law enforcement purposes.

All of this is perfectly legal, and only in limited circumstances—such as when government or law enforcement agencies seeks to unmask the identity of a person through his or her cellphone ID—do the authorities have to get a court warrant. The cellphone data itself is a commodity and can be purchased in the open market. It tells precisely where we are, and by tracking this information over time, competent investigators can develop a "pattern of life" showing our movements throughout a given period—an hour, a day, a week, or even longer.

Using geotracking, for example, someone could figure out that I was home last night, then stopped at Starbucks on my way to the studio to record my podcast, after which I made a trip to the bank and the grocery store before having lunch at a local Italian restaurant. Indeed, more elaborate geotracking would reveal my regular weekday routine, including any break from that routine, such as a trip to give a speech or a weekend getaway with Debbie. By disclosing my locations in time, my phone gives away a lot about who I am and what I do, and it does this even while it's turned off. The only way for me to prevent this is to stop carrying my phone around or to throw it away.

In a December 2019 article, the *New York Times* illustrated the power of geotracking by obtaining, from a single data location company, a file showing the locations and movements of some 12 million Americans in major cities over a period of several months. The *Times* could identify specific phones as they moved through beachfront neighborhoods in California, in secure facilities like the Pentagon, in the Eisenhower Executive Office Building and the West Wing of the White House, and at Mar-a-Lago, Donald Trump's Palm Beach resort.

"One search turned up more than a dozen people visiting the Playboy Mansion, some overnight. Without much effort we spotted visitors to the estates of Johnny Depp, Tiger Woods and Arnold Schwarzenegger. . . . We followed military officials with security clearances as they drove home at night. We tracked law enforcement officers as they took their kids to school." During Trump's inauguration, the *Times* was able to track

elite attendees at presidential ceremonies, religious observers at church services, supporters assembling across the National Mall. . . .

Protesters were tracked just as rigorously. After the pings of Trump supporters, basking in victory, vanished from the National Mall on Friday evening, they were replaced hours later by those of participants in the Women's March, as a crowd of nearly half a million descended on the capital. . . . Pings at the protest connected to clear trails through the data, documenting the lives of protesters in the months before and after the protest, including where they lived and worked.[9]

If you're getting the idea that we have very limited privacy as a consequence of our cellphones, you're right. Remarkably, we give up our rights to privacy simply by clicking on various links. Catherine Engelbrecht drew my attention to one of those little disclaimers—you know, the ones that hardly anyone bothers to read. This one is from the *Daily Mail*'s very popular website:

"We and our partners process, store and access data such as IP address, unique ID and browsing data based on your consent to display personalized ads and content, ad and content measurement, audience insights and product development, use precise geolocation data, and actively scan device characteristics for identification." And then the kicker: "Sometimes we and our partners don't rely on your consent but rely on legitimate interest to process your data." In other words, you are giving us your consent, but even if you don't, we're grabbing your data.

But why would the *Daily Mail* and other sites like it want your data? The short answer is: to sell you stuff. Not only can the newspaper tell from the data whom its readers are and what they do, but it can also tell where they shop and what types of products and advertising might appeal to them. Moreover, the newspaper can very profitably sell that data to various retailers who can use it for promotional and advertising purposes. It's big business.

Ever get a notification on your phone when you are at a store telling you the merchant is having a special on this or that? Debbie and I were in the mall recently, and as we approached the Apple store Debbie got a notification on her phone from, you guessed it, Apple. At other times, we've been in stores like CVS and received notifications about discounts and specials available at that location at that time. If you've gotten some of these and wondered how these stores could possibly know where you are, well, now you know. They know because they are geotracking you.

Geotracking is most commonly used for commerce. It's called "location-based marketing" or "ecommerce marketing." When companies identify potential customers in a geographical region they are doing "geo-targeting." When they construct a zone or circle to find out who's in the vicinity of a local business, that's "geo-fencing." I came across an advertising site that boasts about the prospects of "geo-conquesting," which refers to the practice of businesses luring customers away from the competition. If customers are going near a competitor's store, you blast them with discounts and promotional content through push notifications directly to their phones, inviting them to your store instead.[10]

Geotracking is also now routinely used for intelligence and law enforcement. In an early use of this technology, geotracking was used to identify the location of Osama bin Laden at the Abbottabad compound in Pakistan where he was hunted down and killed. Bin Laden himself didn't use a cellphone, but his associates did, and U.S. intelligence officials used the cellphone data to find bin Laden and also to develop an idea of the pattern of life at the compound—who came, who went, who was responsible for security, and so on.[11]

The FBI also used geotracking to identify, locate, and arrest January 6 protesters who went inside the Capitol. *Wired* broke the story, which it titled "How a Secret Google Geofence Warrant Helped Catch the

Capitol Riot Mob." According to the article, investigators asked Google to identify any smartphone inside the Capitol on January 6. They then compiled an exclusion list of phones owned by people who were authorized to be there. Everyone else became a criminal suspect.

The investigative report noted that the FBI served two geofence warrants on Google even as the protesters were inside the Capitol. Then, according to the article, the FBI was able to secure court permission to unmask the individuals through their cellphone IDs. In virtually no time, authorities had their physical addresses, email addresses, and phone numbers.[12] In effect, the protesters' phones proved to be the digital spies that gave them away.

This interesting tale—which *Wired* trumpeted as the consequence of a months-long investigation, but which was more likely leaked to the publication by the FBI itself—is accurate in revealing the capabilities of modern geotracking, but it should not be taken entirely at face value. Gregg Phillips told me that his team has carefully studied the arrests made in the aftermath of January 6, and some of them were made too soon for the geotracking to have yielded results.

Geotracking takes time, Gregg explained, as it involves building patterns of life, then getting court warrants to unmask the suspects, then tracking down their current locations to arrest them. In the case of a whole bunch of January 6 suspects who were arrested almost immediately following the event, there simply wasn't enough time. Gregg says that if geotracking was involved in their cases, the FBI must have been tracking them *before* January 6.

●🎥

While geotracking is a tool with obvious benefits for law enforcement, it is expensive and time-consuming to do this work. It also requires technical expertise. Remarkably, many local law enforcement agencies don't have this expertise, and some don't have the resources. Also, geotracking is relatively new, so old-style detectives might simply be unaccustomed to using it even in cases where it could be helpful.

As Gregg Phillips and his team dug into the geotracking data in Georgia, they found a pattern of election fraud that was shocking in its magnitude—with hundreds of provable felonies—coordinated by nonprofit institutions acting like a criminal network or cartel, engaged in the business of stealing an election that would alter the political balance of power in the country.

Consequently, Gregg and Catherine notified Georgia governor Brian Kemp, Georgia secretary of state Brad Raffensperger, and the Georgia Bureau of Investigation (GBI) of what they had discovered. Yet to their consternation and dismay, they encountered resistance to the idea of opening an official investigation. "They simply sat on what we gave them," Catherine said. "No response."

Why, Gregg and Catherine asked, might this be the case? One possibility is political—a possibility I'll discuss in a later chapter. The other possibility is that the authorities weren't sure about the accuracy of the data. Perhaps this technology was new to them, or at least to those reviewing the True the Vote reports. "We felt that maybe they needed us to validate the data for them," Catherine said, "to show them that this was something they needed to check out, review, and if necessary prosecute."

The two of them had a stroke of genius. "We came up with the idea," Gregg said, "that maybe we could help solve a couple of murders in the area, using precisely the same technology and precisely the same methods." If geotracking could prove its usefulness in solving an unsolved crime or two, the GBI at least might see its value in documenting election fraud at the mail-in drop boxes. To Gregg and Catherine's good fortune, there were two high-profile crimes in the Atlanta area begging to be solved.

The first was the case of Secoriea Turner, an eight-year-old girl shot and killed near a Wendy's restaurant on July 4, 2020, during a Black Lives Matter riot. BLM and Antifa activists had taken over the area in the weeks following the fatal police shooting of Rayshard Brooks. They had burned down the Wendy's where Brooks had been killed and renamed the area Rayshard Brooks Peace Center.

"It was a peaceful protest at first," Derante Wilkins, a local resident told the press, "then people came with guns." The activists confronted journalists and local residents. They made threats. They beat up people who tried to enter their occupied zone. There was even a shooting arising out of a fracas between a black man and a female protester. Yet city officials and police did nothing, in effect relinquishing control of the area to the armed mob. This phenomenon of militarized occupation has also been seen in other cities like Portland and Seattle.

Secoriea Turner's mom, Charmaine Turner, drove her Jeep unwittingly into this occupied zone, and when she tried to turn her vehicle around, multiple shots were fired at her car and her little girl was killed. The crime was unsolved. Despite pleas from Turner and others for witnesses to come forward, no one did.

"You killed your own—you killed your own this time," Secoriea's father, Secoriya Williamson, said at a news conference. "We deserve justice," Charmaine Turner said. "Someone needs to be held accountable." Yet if there were any racial activists or social justice warriors who knew who had fired the shots, they weren't telling.

Police arrested one man, Julian Conley, based on a video recording that put him at the scene of the crime, but he said he had merely witnessed the shooting. The authorities confirmed through further inquiries that there were at least two shooters, and admitted they were still trying to identify the perpetrators. A year later, the crime remained unsolved.[13]

During my interview with Gregg Phillips for the film 2000 *Mules*, Gregg unfurled a map of the area. His geotracking data showed the location and movement of every cellphone in the period preceding, during, and immediately after the shooting. Obviously there were dozens of cellphones, including the one in Turner's Jeep. But, said Gregg, when you consider where the shots came from, the angle of the shots, and the timing, two devices stand out as being where the shooters would have been.

Now, Gregg said, watch the movement of the two devices. Following the shooting, one of them moves rapidly across the street to dissolve into a larger group, while the other scoots to an overpass and then pauses, the owner of the device presumably hiding under the overarching road. "This calls for further investigation," Gregg said, "but here, I believe, are the two prime suspects." He didn't know their names, but he did have their cellphone IDs, which he turned over to the FBI.

In mid-August 2021, two black men were formally charged with the murder of Secoriea Turner. One was Julian Conley, the man originally arrested in connection with the shooting. The other was Jerrion McKinney, allegedly a fellow member with Conley of the Bloods gang. According to the charging documents, they were participants in the BLM riot and had fired into the Jeep when Turner entered without authorization their so-called occupied zone.[14]

Gregg and Catherine are very cautious about their role in this case. They cannot say for sure—because the FBI isn't saying—whether the geotracking data was instrumental in nailing the suspects. But the FBI has maintained its contact with Catherine and Gregg, and it seems reasonable to conclude that their information was helpful in assisting the authorities.

Now let's turn to the second case. On July 28, 2021, Katie Janness was stabbed to death along with her dog Bowie in Piedmont Park in

Atlanta. The sheer brutality of the crime—Janness was stabbed more than fifty times in her face, neck, and midsection; her throat was slashed; and the letters FAT were etched into her body—suggested a personal motive. But this was merely a supposition.

Janness, a lesbian, had told her fiancée, Emma Clark, that she was going out to walk her dog. When Janness failed to return, Clark used a phone app to trace Janness's location. Note the accuracy of the app; it took her straight to the scene of the crime. She found both Janness and Bowie dead at the entrance to the park at around 1:00 a.m. Since nothing was taken—Janness's phone, headphones, and keys were found at the scene of the crime—robbery did not appear to be a motive.

The FBI joined local law enforcement to investigate, but months later, the crime remained unsolved. There were surveillance cameras in the park, but they offered little evidence. One camera showed Janness and the dog going through a rainbow crosswalk at Tenth Street and Piedmont Avenue, but that was it. There were no witnesses and no suspects.[15]

Gregg Phillips and his team reviewed the geotracking data for the park on the night of the murder. They identified three cellphones in the immediate vicinity of the killing. One was Janness's phone. The other two were unidentified. But Gregg was able to ascertain that one of the other devices was from out of state. Had someone, then, come in from out of town to commit the murder?

The other device was local. What Gregg found very interesting is that the device could also be seen, on more than one occasion, in the parking lot of Janness's apartment building. It seemed like someone had been watching Janness, possibly to figure out her daily routine. Gregg believed one of these two devices belonged to the murderer.

Pulling back and taking in a wider radius, Gregg found several other cellphone devices in the park around the time of the murder. None of them seemed close enough to have witnessed the murder, but the authorities would certainly want to interview them because they might have seen something relevant to the case. Again, Gregg and Catherine turned over their findings to the authorities and, as I write, the authorities believe they are closer to solving the case.[16]

Gregg and Catherine investigated these cases in exactly the same manner that they have investigated election fraud. The geotracking works in precisely the same way, tracking cellphones present at the scene of the crime. Geotracking is similar to DNA or fingerprint evidence; only it points to particular cellphones rather than directly to their owners, though that link can be made through further investigation.

As we'll see, what Gregg and Catherine established is that by using this new and reliable technology, we can now learn about the massive and coordinated election fraud operation in the five critical states that determined the 2020 election.

CHAPTER 4

Herd of Mules

It doesn't take a lot of votes to flip an election. At least, that proved to be the case in 2020. Let's look at the vote margins in five states. Michigan: 154,000 votes. Pennsylvania: 80,000 votes. Wisconsin: 20,000 votes. Georgia: 12,000 votes. Arizona: 10,000 votes. Biden won all these states. Yet if he had lost them, he would have lost the election. To flip these states is to flip the Electoral College, and to flip the Electoral College is to flip the country. The factual question True the Vote set out to investigate is: Did Biden really win them? In this chapter we will answer that question.

The same question applies to the Senate runoff election in Georgia. Democrats in early 2021 narrowly defeated two incumbent GOP senators, David Perdue and Kelly Loeffler, which delivered to them control of the U.S. Senate in addition to the presidency. Since Democrats controlled the House, albeit narrowly, they had effective control of the entire legislative and executive branches. But again, the question is whether this result in Georgia was achieved lawfully. We are now in a position to find out.

Since True the Vote's investigation focused on mules engaged in paid ballot trafficking, let's begin by clarifying what ballot trafficking is and where and why it's illegal. Ballot trafficking is the practice of casting absentee or mail-in ballots without voter authorization. It is also the practice of accepting payment for a ballot. If voters are paid for voting—or voting a particular way—or mules are paid for delivering votes, those votes are fraudulent and the participants in the scheme are guilty of a serious crime.

Ballot trafficking as defined here is illegal in every state. It is not the same as vote harvesting, which is legal in some states. (Election laws are made at the state level and vary considerably from state to state.) Vote harvesting is the collection of absentee or mail-in ballots by a third party who then drops them in a mailbox or delivers them to election officials. Twenty-seven states permit vote harvesting, although even these states typically specify who may and may not return ballots, generally allowing the privilege to family members and caregivers but denying it to employers, union representatives, candidates, or campaign workers.

In California and Hawaii, which have the most liberal vote-harvesting laws in the country, you can hand over your ballot to a third party with virtually no restrictions, and that third party can either mail the collected ballots or deliver them. But even these states prohibit compensation for collecting and casting the ballots. California law defines compensation as any form of monetary payment, goods, services, benefits, promises, offers of employment, or any other form of consideration offered to another person in exchange for returning a voter's absentee or mail-in ballot.

New Hampshire permits your vote to be delivered by a family member or, if you are in a resident care facility, a staff member. New Jersey allows a bearer designated by the voter to return a vote, but it must be done in person and the bearer must provide proof of identity when delivering a ballot. Minnesota lets voters choose a designated agent to deliver a ballot, but no agent can return more than three ballots in any election. In Alaska, a designated representative can deliver your ballot for you only if you are disabled or qualify for a special-needs ballot.

Now let's look at the five states in question, where Biden's margin of victory was narrow and where the laws are much more restrictive. Arizona specifies that only a family member, household member, or caregiver can return or mail another person's ballot. In Georgia, it's the same with the added proviso that a jail employee can return a ballot on behalf of a voter in custody. In Pennsylvania and Wisconsin, only the voter can return the ballot; there are no provisions to turn ballots over to third parties, not even close relatives. Pennsylvania makes a small exception for a disabled voter, who can designate someone else to return his or her ballot on the condition that the person signs an affidavit that he has not altered the ballot in any way.

Michigan is a tricky case. The law in that state specifies that only immediate family members can deliver a ballot to the clerk for the voter. Yet in 2020 a judge authorized vote harvesting, and two weeks passed before the judge's decision was overturned. The practical consequence was that vote harvesting was illegal in Michigan, then legal for two weeks during the early voting period, then illegal again. But again—paying mules, or anyone for that matter, to deliver votes is always illegal.[1]

With limited resources, True the Vote decided to focus on key urban areas in just five states. These areas were the greater Atlanta area, which encompasses Fulton, Gwinnett, DeKalb, and Cobb Counties; two areas in Arizona, the greater Phoenix area, mostly in Maricopa County, and Yuma County; the greater Detroit area, Wayne County, Michigan; the Milwaukee area of Wisconsin; and the greater Philadelphia area in Pennsylvania. In effect, Catherine and Gregg decided to test the hypothesis that you can steal an election by stealing just a handful of counties in five swing states.

True the Vote constructed geofences around these key areas and purchased the entire database of cellphone traffic for the period of early voting through Election Day. Altogether, the data set included 10 trillion location-based cell signals. Catherine and Gregg's focus was the movement of cellphones between designated nonprofit centers—homeless shelters, non-governmental organizations (NGOs), left-wing churches, activist organizations—and mail-in ballot drop boxes.

There is nothing suspicious, obviously, in a person from one of those organizations, or someone who stopped by one of those organizations, going to a drop box. They could be depositing their own ballot or that of a family member. It becomes problematic, however, when the same cellphone can be located on the same night visiting multiple drop boxes. And if there's a pattern of the same individual's stopping by multiple nonprofit organizations and subsequently delivering ballots to multiple drop boxes, that's illegal ballot trafficking. There is no innocent explanation for that behavior.

True the Vote's investigation began in Georgia, where a whistleblower came forward and admitted that he had made $45,000 trafficking 4,500 votes at $10 apiece. Quoting from True the Vote's complaint submitted November 30, 2021, to Georgia secretary of state Brad Raffensperger:

> True the Vote's contracted team of researchers and investigator spoke with several individuals regarding person knowledge, methods and organizations involved in ballot trafficking in Georgia. One such individual, hereafter referred to as John Doe, admitted to personally participating and provided specific information about the ballot

trafficking process. This information was provided under agreement of anonymity.

John Doe described a network of non-governmental organizations (NGOs) that worked together to facilitate a ballot trafficking scheme in Georgia. John Doe claimed to have been one of many individuals paid to collect and deliver absentee ballots during the early voting periods of the November 2020 general election and the January 2021 runoff election. While acknowledging that others might view his actions as inappropriate, John Doe did not seem to understand the unlawful nature of this conduct nor that it might constitute organized criminal activity. John Doe's perception was that he had been hired to do a job and it was appropriate to be paid for the services rendered.

John Doe's assignment included collecting ballots, both from voters in targeted neighborhoods and from NGOs that had their own ballot collection processes, delivering those ballots to other NGOs, picking up designated ballot bundles from the same group of NGOs, and depositing ballots into drop boxes spanning six counties in the metro Atlanta area. Each drop box delivery would typically include between 5 to 20 ballots. John Doe described a payment validation process which involved taking cell phone pictures of the drop box where ballots were deposited. Participants were compensated, typically at a rate of $10 per ballot. John Doe stated he had been paid directly by one of these NGOs.[2]

Evidently Raffensperger's investigators are trying to find John Doe. Knowing they are looking for him, John Doe has gone underground. He made it clear from the outset that he didn't want to be part of any criminal investigation because of the dangers it would pose to him, both of criminal prosecution and, even if he made a deal with the state, of being targeted by the other mules, who now stand to be exposed and prosecuted, and by the criminal enterprise that hired him in the first place.

Yet while this mule refused to come forward publicly, he did meet several times with True the Vote investigators, and he did help the organization to formulate its methodology for its five-state investigation. Based on what Gregg and Catherine had learned in Yuma, Arizona, and what the Georgia whistleblower told them, they had an idea of how the mule operation worked and what to look for.

So the group's investigation began in Georgia and then moved on to Arizona, Wisconsin, Michigan, and Pennsylvania. True the Vote decided to focus only on the egregious cases, mules stopping by multiple activist organizations and going to at least ten drop boxes. This obviously meant they would undercount the magnitude of fraudulent votes, but they decided to focus on clear violations in counties that could have changed the electoral outcome.

I conducted a detailed interview with Catherine and Gregg for the movie *2000 Mules*. Because of the constraints of time, however, only a small part of that interview could be used in the movie; I'm going to tap into that interview in much more detail in this chapter and the next. We started by discussing the geotracking evidence.

Dinesh: What was your hypothesis, Catherine, as you and Gregg began this research?

Catherine: The hypothesis was, if you're going to cheat, how would you go about this in a way that would be provable, trackable, traceable? And we decided to let the data tell the tale.

Dinesh: How did you get your hands on this data?

Gregg: We bought it.

Dinesh: Tell us about the places you bought data for and what you were looking for, and what's the time period?

Gregg: We bought from October 1 through the election to pick up any early voting that might have occurred, especially in these drop boxes. In Georgia, we actually bought from October 1 through January 6 after the runoff.

Catherine: Georgia was interesting because we got two bites at the apple.

Gregg: We decided to go the Atlanta metro area—the drop boxes in the area. We fenced around those. We created similar fences around some of the organizations that had come in through the hotline—through witnesses that had seen things they were uncomfortable with. Then we were able to purchase data of people that had been near those drop boxes and also near those organizations. This way, we were able to skinny it down to about 500,000 phones in the initial buy. Across the country, we bought 10 trillion signals.

Dinesh: What was the criterion that you set to say, "Let's search for this."

Gregg: This was a major effort conducted by twelve of the best people in America, and even in the world, in this work. So the final decision was, they had to have been to ten or more drop boxes. Meaning unique visits inside of a space and five or more visits to one or more of these organizations.

Catherine: When you look at the data as a whole, as Gregg just defined those variables, those were the outliers. And you saw it in state after state, location after location, that just sort of broke apart as traveling in ways that are distinctive.

Dinesh: What you're saying, it seems to me, is that there's no reason for someone to go to even two drop boxes, but maybe there's a conceivable reason someone did that. Let's identify a large number of drop boxes and multiple trips and that way we're going to catch not all the offenders, but the worst offenders.

Gregg: We want to absolutely ensure that we don't have false positives, meaning including people that should not have been included. On the other hand, we wanted to reduce, if we could, the number of false negatives, in other words, not including someone that should have been included.

Dinesh: You've laid out a geotracking map, and on it I see dots, I see circles, I see blue. What's the significance of everything on the map?

Gregg: We create a visual, a pattern of life that someone can see and look at, rather than a whole spreadsheet of numbers. What you see here is a single person, on a single day, in Atlanta, Georgia.

Dinesh: What are the orange dots?

Gregg: Those are drop boxes.

Dinesh: And the circles, I take it, reflect the nonprofit centers?

Gregg: The stash houses, as Catherine calls them. Where the ballots are collected, bucketed, and handed to the mules to take to the drop boxes.

Dinesh: And what's the blue, the blue tracks?

Gregg: That's a smoothed-out pattern of life so that we could take the movement of the individual cellphone signals and marry them into something that's visual so you can see the movement of the individual. This guy went to five organizations and twenty-eight drop boxes in six counties in one day.

Dinesh: Wow.

Gregg: What's interesting about this particular one—it was the first time we had seen someone go across multiple counties, making hard stops at the five organizations. And then again, it wasn't as though they were just driving by on the highway and stopping. To get to some of these drop boxes, you had to be intentional. You had to get off the highway. You had to go on surface streets, you had to turn in somewhere, in order to get to many of these drop boxes. And this was one of the very first graphics we created in Atlanta. To our team, it was the graphic that made us say, okay, we got this.

•☞

Dinesh: Moving to the big picture, what did you find in Georgia?

Gregg: We're not in any way saying this is all there is. We're saying that just based on our criteria, we identified in Atlanta 242 people that went to an average of 24 drop boxes and 8 organizations during a 2-week period.

Dinesh: The organizations—is that where they get the ballots?

Catherine: Yes, and then they go on routes. Which is also significant, because one of the questions that comes up in the work we've done is, well, how do you know that this wasn't just somebody that's got a big family and they just deposited a bunch of ballots once? Or how do you know that this person didn't just work at a location that is near a drop box so they're constantly going by a drop box? And so the elements that are additive here—the going to the nonprofits, the ability to identify the pattern of approach to a drop box, and that's not going past a drop box but directly to a drop box and then back to another point, and then to another drop box.

Dinesh: Isn't the timing significant? If some guy's going to a drop box at 2:00 a.m., presumably he's not out for a walk.

Catherine: Right.

Dinesh: We started out with Georgia, where you identified, in Atlanta alone, 242 mules. Now let's go over to Arizona. You did a similar buy.

Gregg: We bought two places in Arizona. We bought Yuma County and we bought Maricopa County.

Dinesh: Did you use the same criteria in Arizona, or were the criteria different?

Gregg: It was a little bit different. For instance, in Maricopa County they had drive-through drop boxes. And that presented a whole different manner of checking on this. So there are differences in how we process, but from a purchase perspective, it was close to the same. Proportionally, interestingly, the numbers came out close to the same.

Dinesh: How many mules in Arizona?

Gregg: A little over 200. In Phoenix alone.

Dinesh: And again, you say with the difference—this guy's walking, this guy's driving—but you're measuring the same pattern of behavior?

Gregg: We are.

Dinesh: I think this is all very significant, because these were very close states, right?

Gregg: Yes, very close.

Dinesh: Then you moved on to . . .

Gregg: Wisconsin. We took a look mostly in Milwaukee. The gross numbers were a little down, but the average number of visits to the drop boxes was up. So we had over a hundred in Milwaukee County, or in the city of Milwaukee. Fewer mules, but far more drop boxes. So the mules themselves were more prolific at the drop boxes. Instead of four unique visits to each drop box, I think we averaged twenty-eight in Wisconsin.

Dinesh: I've heard people in Milwaukee are really hard-working, and maybe they just went overtime.

Catherine: Overachievers.

Dinesh: Let's go to Michigan.

Gregg: The numbers are really amping up. We have more than 500 mules that we've identified in Michigan. Again—the number of boxes is lower.

Dinesh: Where in Michigan?

Gregg: Detroit, mainly.

Catherine: Wayne County.

Gregg: And the number of boxes is fewer, so the number of visits per box is higher. We have people in Detroit that went to more than 100 drop boxes.

Dinesh: This is stunning, because I cannot think of a rational or innocent reason for someone to do that. It just doesn't exist.

Catherine: Right.

Dinesh: So I'm running a bit of math in my head. We've got 500 or so mules in Michigan. I'm adding them up from Georgia, Wisconsin, Arizona. I'm up to about 1,000 mules. Let's go to Pennsylvania. A critical state. I think it was Pennsylvania that really gave Biden the election, in the sense that it tipped over to Biden. The deal was done. What have you found in Pennsylvania?

Gregg: I have no doubt that if we expanded in Pennsylvania it would produce mind-numbing results. But in Philadelphia alone, we've identified more than 1,100 mules, at rates well beyond anything else we'd seen. Closer to 50 ballot drop boxes each.

Dinesh: Each guy going to 50 drop boxes?

Gregg: It's extraordinary. The depth of what appears to be cheating in Philadelphia is extraordinary. We saw insane things, like people driving back and forth—these mules—driving back and forth to New Jersey across the bridge.

Dinesh: So you're saying the origin point appears to be Jersey. Now running 1,100 mules times 50, we're at 50,000 drop box visits by mules in Philadelphia alone, or the greater Philadelphia area. Is there a way to estimate, even roughly, how many ballots are being tossed into a box at a given time?

Gregg: We've simulated, we've looked at it. They're actually pretty sophisticated. They're not going up and dumping in buckets full of ballots.

Catherine: The idea is to stay under the radar. We believe that's why we see these routes being followed. The number is three, five, ten ballots. It's not going to be extreme. But then, they're not done for the day either. They're going place to place to place, day upon day upon day.

Dinesh: Now, adding these numbers up, we have 2,000-plus mules. Given the number of drop boxes that each of them used, and considering the multiple visits they made to each drop box, are we talking about margins here that could potentially swing these states?

Gregg: Yes.

Dinesh: So, in other words, the mules alone, and the amount of vote trafficking, could have swung the state of Georgia the other way?

Gregg: Yes.

Dinesh: And Arizona?

Gregg: Yes.

Dinesh: And Michigan?

Gregg: Yes.

Dinesh: And Wisconsin?

Gregg: Yes.

Dinesh: And Pennsylvania?

Gregg: Especially Pennsylvania. This was an organized effort to subvert a free and fair election. This is organized crime. You can't look at this data in its aggregate and believe anything otherwise.

*

It's useful to get an idea of the magnitude of the theft in just these five states and compare it to the difference between Trump and Biden in those states. There are a couple of different ways to estimate the volume of stolen or fraudulent votes. The first—which is the narrow way—is simply to compute the number in each state based on the number of highly active mules identified in that state. These are the mules that went to ten or more drop boxes and also to several non-profit vote stash houses to pick up the ballots. Let's call this Model 1.

The other—more sophisticated—way is to create a model that estimates the number of illegally trafficked votes in the whole state. This model recognizes that the mule population is substantially greater than the subset of top offenders: if there are mules who went to ten or more drop boxes, there were likely mules who went to fewer than ten drop boxes. So Model 2 seeks to approximate the total amount of election fraud counting all the mules.

Let's start with Model 1 and do the math on the 2,000 mules. The average number of drop boxes for each mule varies by state, but the average for the five states in question is 38. As for the number of illegal votes deposited in each drop box, it seems to vary between 3 and 10, so let's use the middle number 5. Multiplying these out, we get 76,000 mule visits to drop boxes in the key states generating, at 5 votes per visit, 380,000 illegal votes. That's the most conservative estimate of the volume of fraud in the monitored regions of the five swing states.

By running these numbers state by state, we can see how, by themselves, these 2,000 mules had a potentially decisive impact on the election. (I'm rounding the numbers to make the math easy to comprehend.) In Michigan, True the Vote counted 500 mules making 50 drop box visits apiece. This adds up to 25,000 drop box visits. Multiplying by 5, we get 125,000 trafficked votes, a big number, but still smaller than the 154,000-vote margin between Biden and Trump in that state. So in this calculation Michigan with its 16 electoral votes stays in the Biden column.

In Wisconsin, True the Vote found more than 100 mules making 28 drop box visits each. That's 2,800 drop box visits, which at 5 votes apiece adds up to 14,000 illegal votes. That's 6,000 votes short of the 20,000-vote difference between the two candidates. So Wisconsin, too, remains, albeit very narrowly, in Biden's column. Biden hangs on to Wisconsin's 10 electoral votes.

Next, Georgia. True the Vote found roughly 250 mules making 24 drop box visits per mule. At 5 ballots per box, that's 30,000 illegally trafficked votes, far more than the 12,000-vote difference between Trump and Biden. So Georgia with its 16 electoral votes moves over into the Trump column. In Arizona, the numbers are roughly the same. More than 200 mules making 20-plus drop box visits yielding, at 5 ballots per drop, 20,000 illegal votes. Again, these illegal votes are substantially more than the 10,000-vote margin that gave the state's electoral votes to Biden. Trump wins Arizona and its 11 electoral votes.

In Philadelphia, we have more than 1,100 mules making 50 drop box visits each, generating 275,000 illegal votes—again, comfortably exceeding the 80,000-vote margin between Trump and Biden. So Pennsylvania with its 20 electoral votes goes for Trump, and modifying the electoral vote count based on these 3 flipped states, Pennsylvania would have given the election to Trump, 279 electoral votes to Biden's 259.

Remember: This is the narrowest way of looking at the fraud, and even here, Trump wins. But no one thinks that our 2,000 mules were the only mules trafficking illegal votes. Gregg and his team decided to widen their search algorithm to get a fuller picture of the election fraud in the five key states. They reduced the number of drop boxes from ten or more to five or more, an effort aimed at catching not merely the most egregious mules but also the normal, or less industrious, mules.

This new search caused the number of cellphone devices—which is to say, the number of mules—to rise dramatically.

In Wisconsin, there were 5,571 mules. In Georgia, 6,178. In Arizona, 13,829. In Pennsylvania, 13,967. In Michigan, 15,106. The total number of mules in the five states based on this expanded search criterion: 54,651. This is an astounding number because it means that a huge number of fraudsters were involved in this coordinated scheme. My movie and book are both titled *2000 Mules*, but that, as it turns out, is a ridiculous underestimate of the total number of mules.

Gregg and his team then used a very conservative estimate for the average number of ballots per drop: 3. Running the math—number of mules times 5 drop box visits per mule times 3 ballots per drop—we get 83,565 illegal votes in Wisconsin, 92,670 in Georgia, 209,505 in Pennsylvania, 226,590 in Michigan, and 207,435 in Arizona. The total number of illegal votes in the five states: 819,765. Even this is an undercount, because the search criterion was for 5 *or more* drop boxes, but we assume that each mule went to just five.

When Gregg and his team reviewed their numbers, they spotted an interesting pattern, which becomes clear when you divide the number of illegally trafficked votes in each swing state by the total number of mail-in ballots in that state. In Wisconsin, 6.55 percent of mail-in ballots were fraudulently delivered by our mules; in Arizona, 7.19 percent; in Georgia, 7.02 percent; in Michigan, 7.97 percent; in Pennsylvania, 7.97 percent. We see here a fairly consistent pattern: around 7 percent of all mail-in ballots in these states were generated through illegal ballot trafficking.

Using this fuller and more thorough calculation of illegal ballot trafficking, the numbers are large enough to have given all the five states to Trump. In this scenario, Trump would have won the electoral vote 305 to 233. Basically, the electoral vote count would be reversed. Instead of the official 2020 election numbers, Biden 306 and Trump

232, we get Trump 305, Biden 233. This evidence acquired by True the Vote shows coordinated fraud on a giant scale, unprecedented in a presidential election.

The cheating—let's be very clear on this—is for one side, the Democrats. The cheating was to put Joe Biden into the White House. It is easy to feign ignorance about this, with claims like, "Yes, Dinesh, but since we can't dive in and separate the illegal votes from the legal votes, how do we know which side did this? For all you know it could have been the Republicans." There are four separate reasons why this argument falls flat.

First, the activist and nonprofit groups the mules went to were all on the Democratic Left. It defies logic to say that these groups are doing vote trafficking for the Republican Party. These are not MAGA organizations. Rather, they are organizations with names like Chicanos Por La Causa and Comite De Bien Estar and Race Forward and Asian Americans Advancing Justice and the New Georgia Project and the League of Women Voters and the National Education Association. They have a known ideological bent and deep affiliations with the cultural Left and the Democratic Party.

Second, there is a considerable overlap between the mule population and activists who took part in Antifa and Black Lives Matter riots. There was an Antifa-BLM riot in Atlanta in the weeks leading up to the 2020 election. There were also Antifa-BLM riots and demonstrations in the other swing states and across the country. Is it possible, Gregg Phillips wondered, to match the mules with these Antifa-BLM activists and criminals?

Turns out it is possible. There's a nonprofit organization, the Armed Conflict Location and Event Data Project (ACLED), that operates worldwide. From Pakistan to Somalia to the United States, the group tracks the dates, times, locations, and characteristics of all violent protests around the world. The objective is to provide law enforcement with tools to compare these events and see if there are connections between the groups and individuals that participate in these violent activities. It's a valuable anti-terrorism database.

Well, then. Gregg decided to compare the cellphone IDs of his 242 mules in Atlanta with the cellphone IDs of the violent rioters in the ACLED database. "Sure enough," he told me, "there are dozens and dozens of our mules in these databases. In fact, one-third of our Atlanta mules took part in the Antifa-BLM riots."

There are similar overlaps for the mules in the other states. Gregg estimates that between 10 and 23 percent of all mules identified in the five jurisdictions are also on the ACLED list. So these are bad guys, many of them with criminal backgrounds, and they are all on the political Left. The mules, in other words, are part of the criminal wing of the Democratic Party.

Third, it was the Democrats who created the infrastructure of cheating—as I'll show in detail later—with "get out the vote" efforts that amounted to sending out the mules.

The final proof is in the pudding: Which side won, narrowly, in these states? It's quite clear the cheaters knew where they had to cheat and how much, and they did a lot of cheating to provide their candidate with a sufficient margin to win in every one of the five swing states that would determine the outcome of the election.

CHAPTER 5

Caught in the Act

Geotracking evidence is powerful, but it always helps to have video to prove innocence or guilt. In some cases—like that of Kyle Rittenhouse—juries can exonerate a defendant based upon what they see. Rittenhouse might be in prison today, convicted of murder, if it hadn't been for the video evidence that showed his innocence.

Video evidence is highly relevant in electoral fraud cases. In his report to the Wisconsin State Assembly, retired state supreme court justice Michael Gableman used video evidence to expose electoral fraud in Wisconsin nursing homes. Gableman vetted nursing homes in five counties and found voter participation rates of 95 to 100 percent. Virtually every confined resident voted! These rates were markedly higher than in previous elections. Could it be, then, that there were markedly higher levels of excitement about the 2020 race among the ninety thousand or so residents of Wisconsin nursing homes?

Actually, no. Gableman showed—and this was the power of the video evidence—that many of these residents were incapable of voting. Gableman interviewed nursing home residents on video, showing that some were unable to make rational or coherent decisions. Some had been adjudicated incompetent and were thus ineligible to vote. One resident had not been of sound mind for more than ten years. Another had been institutionalized since the 1970s and had never previously voted. Yet Gableman found that all these residents had voted in the 2020 election—or, far more likely, someone had filled out ballots in their names and voted on their behalf.[1]

Yet while video evidence is critical, that doesn't mean it is going to be available. The election rules prepared by the Cybersecurity and Infrastructure Security Agency (CISA), which provides "guidance for state, local, tribal and territorial election officials on how to administer and secure election infrastructure in light of the Covid-19 epidemic," clearly state that all mail-in drop boxes should have good security, be well-lighted twenty-four hours a day, and have security cameras. When drop boxes are unstaffed, the rules say, they should have, in addition to proper decals branding them and security seals to prevent tampering, video surveillance cameras and media storage devices to preserve the recorded video.[2]

Yet even though CISA makes it clear that video surveillance is important for ensuring election security and integrity, many counties—indeed most in the five states we are considering—simply ignored this guidance. This alone puts into question CISA's own insistence after the fact that the 2020 election was the most secure in U.S. history. CISA has no basis for making this claim, which is dubious on its face and rendered close to absurd given the geotracking evidence offered in the last chapter and the video evidence we will cover in this one.

True the Vote made a concerted effort through open records requests to obtain video surveillance footage in the five states covered in its investigation. In every state, the group encountered resistance. After persistent efforts in Georgia, True the Vote obtained an estimated

15–20 percent of the surveillance video requested in the counties of Fulton, DeKalb, Cobb, and Gwinnett. It's interesting to see what a hassle it is for an independent group to obtain footage that is required under Section 5 of Georgia's State Elections Board rules.

On June 21, 2021, True the Vote asked Fulton County to provide all drop box surveillance video recorded during the 2020 election. In its response, Fulton County informed Catherine that "all available ballot locations stored recordings only go back to October 30, 2020–November 5, 2020, with the exception of Dogwood Library." Further, "the estimated cost would be between $25,00–30,000" and "it will take an estimated 6 months to complete this request."

Catherine and Gregg puzzled over the fact that Fulton's videos merely covered October 30 to November 5. Why was that? Early voting in Georgia began on Monday, October 12. So where was the video from October 1 to October 30? Fulton seemed to be saying it didn't have any. The implication was that the older video had been deleted, even though federal law says that election materials must be held and available for review for twenty-two months. When True the Vote demanded an explanation for the lack of video going back to when early voting started, the Fulton County Office of the County Attorney replied, "I do not have an explanation I can provide other than they do not exist."

On June 6, 2021, True the Vote asked Gwinnett County to provide all ballot drop box surveillance video. Gwinnett claimed to have fulfilled the request, yet Catherine and Gregg noticed upon paying the administrative fee and reviewing the hard drives that they had not been provided video for numerous drop box locations, including Bogan Park Community Recreation Center, Dacula Park Activity Building, Gwinnett Voter Registration and Election Location, Peachtree Corners Branch Library, and George Pierce Park Community Recreation Center. Despite numerous communications and phone calls, Gwinnett County provided no response and no explanation for why the legally required video had not been provided.

True the Vote couldn't get any video out of officials in Yuma, Arizona; Detroit, Michigan; or Philadelphia. In Maricopa County, Arizona, surveillance cameras were installed but many were inexplicably turned off. The group sought to obtain video in Milwaukee, but only the Village of Brown Deer complied, and it provided video of only one of two drop boxes located at Village Hall.

When Paul Bond of *Newsweek* contacted Milwaukee officials in early March 2022 to inquire about video, they said they had offered True the Vote 900 pages of chain-of-custody records, but they were withholding 15,120 hours of video footage because they did not deem that they were required to provide it under a public records request.[3]

Watching the surveillance video they were able to get, Catherine and Gregg noticed that the quality is poor, lighting is bad, cameras are poorly positioned, and key time frames are sometimes missing. But the video had one undeniable benefit: it was the official video from the states themselves. This was not video that had been taken by True the Vote or supplied to True the Vote by a whistleblower.

The very video that True the Vote supplied me—and that I used in the movie *2000 Mules*—is video the states themselves have. They don't need to get it from us; it's their video. We got it from them. No fact-checkers, however dishonest, can question the authenticity of the video evidence, even if they dispute what the videos actually show or prove.

Moreover, True the Vote had, in total, four million minutes of video, both from the 2020 presidential election and from the 2021 Georgia U.S. Senate runoffs. And if this video seemed impossible to go through frame by frame, Catherine and Gregg had a solution to make their job more manageable. They used the geotracking data in conjunction with the video surveillance. In other words, they used the geotracking data to identify when and where the mules were moving, and then they checked the video to confirm that there they were. Consequently, the geotracking evidence and the video evidence reinforced each other and combined to tell a riveting and incontestable story.

∙ᴥ∙

I want to convey the video evidence through my conversation with Catherine and Gregg. The limitation of this format—the limitation of a book—is I can't *show* you the video evidence. For that, you have to see the film, and you can also check out additional documentation on True the Vote's website, truethevote.org. But my interview with Catherine and Gregg contains careful and detailed descriptions of the videos. So here we go.

Dinesh: It's one thing to have the scientific evidence, which is persuasive on its own merit. But it sure would be nice to have some video evidence, I mean, seeing the guys do it, catching them, so to speak, in the act. This would be icing on the cake. Do you have this video evidence?

Catherine: We do.

Dinesh: How much of it do you have?

Gregg: Four million minutes of surveillance video from around the country.

Dinesh: Now we're talking about official surveillance video of these mail-in drop boxes. How did you get it?

Catherine: You can file an open records request—any citizen can do this. Open records requests are typically directed to the secretaries of state or the local municipality or the city—just depending on the jurisdiction and the way they are organized—you just make a very specific request about what it is you are trying to acquire. And in the case of the videos, it was a very protracted process. It appeared as though maybe the intent was that no one would ever look at this video.

Dinesh: Do you have video in Georgia?

Gregg: We do.

Dinesh: Is it video from the presidential election, the runoff election, or both?

Gregg: Both.

Dinesh: And do you have video from other states?

Gregg: It's spotty. But we have some video from Arizona. We have recently learned in some of our counties that video was specifically turned off on particular drop boxes.

Dinesh: In which state?

Gregg: Arizona. Wisconsin, it turns out, even though the rules required them to have video . . .

Catherine: They did not.

Dinesh: What about Pennsylvania?

Gregg: Pennsylvania is still a question mark. There appears to be some video that may be available. We're working on it.

Dinesh: The disturbing thing to me is, it seems there should be video of every drop box. If you're talking about an election for control of the most powerful country in the world, wouldn't it make sense that all drop boxes—I mean, you can't walk into a store—you have parking lots that have surveillance capabilities.

Catherine: Most people think there is video. In 2020, when these drop boxes were set up coast to coast, part of the guidance that came down from one of the federal agencies, CISA, said if you're going to have drop boxes, these are the guidelines we recommend. And most of the states were very quick to echo that guidance and say, absolutely, we are going to follow the guidance. But they didn't.

Dinesh: And given today's cost of technology, it would not have been that hard to do it.

Catherine: No. The money was not the issue. It was the execution that was lost. Or maybe intentionally overlooked.

Dinesh: You sent me a screenshot, Catherine, where you were requesting video in Georgia and they said the video should exist, but it does not exist, and we can't tell you why it doesn't exist.

Catherine: Sadly we have correspondence like that from a lot of states.

Dinesh: But the video you have—this is not video you came up with. This is the official surveillance video of Georgia?

Catherine: Absolutely.

Dinesh: The secretary of state has this video. He can check it out. He can verify the videos we're playing are 100 percent authentic.

Catherine: Absolutely. What kicks it up a notch in our case is we have the geospatial data to support the video. In the absence of video, the geospatial data is key to decoding what the greater scheme was. But in the case of what we're going to show you now, the ability to match this up tells a much bigger story.

Dinesh: I'm getting excited. Let's see the video.

Gregg: So we've named them all. As we go through some of these, we'll tell you what we call them. We call this first guy Multiple. This particular individual we have in a number of different locations at a number of different times. Notice the brazenness of this guy, even though it's late at night, obviously this is well lit. He knows the cameras are there, and he really doesn't care.

So as this person pulls up, he doesn't even bother parking. Of course, it's the middle of the night, so why would he? Gets out, approaches the box. One of the other things we learned in looking at this video, in applying artificial intelligence and other manners to look at this thing, is the intention. When people walk up with intention to cheat, they look around. They basically walk fairly quickly. They try to stuff them in. They get out of there.

In this case, he drops a few on the ground. He has to pick them up. He bends to pick them up, stuffs them in the ballot box. And then, with some measure of intention, he walks back to his car—sitting in the parking lane. He hustles back and he hustles out of there. So this is what it looks like.

Dinesh: Let's look at another one.

Gregg: We call this one Steeler Girl.

Catherine: That's because she's wearing a Pittsburgh Steelers T-shirt. Interesting thing about this person is the device seems to live in South Carolina. So this person isn't even from Georgia. She was here during both election cycles but is not a resident of the state.

Gregg: What's really interesting to know, for people like us looking at these types of things from a forensics perspective, is a couple of things. First of all, she has on a mask. Which at the time was not terribly unusual. But as she approached the drop box, she never looks at the trash can. Right? And that becomes important later.

Dinesh: She's looking the other way.

Gregg: The other thing is she has surgical gloves on. And what we noticed—what one of our analysts noticed—was these surgical gloves only appeared on our mules from December 23 forward in the runoff. So we didn't see them previous to December 23, and we couldn't figure out why. Then it dawned on us that on December 22 there was an indictment handed down in Arizona, in San Luis, Arizona, for people that had stuffed ballots. And the way the FBI and the attorney general in Arizona nailed them was fingerprints. And the next day, and days forward, the gloves start to show up on the mules.

Dinesh: So this particular video is from the Georgia runoffs. January of '21?

Gregg: That's right.

Catherine: This particular one is at 1:00 in the morning on January the fifth.

Gregg: And so, watch her. Watch what she does. Remember she never looks at the trash can. She walks up with intention. Stuffs her ballots in there. It's like a small stack, maybe three. Maybe four. Takes the gloves off. And then puts them in a trash can that she never looked at.

Dinesh: She knew it was there.

Gregg: She knew it was there. Right. So we have her on a number of locations. We've been able to track in a significant way her pattern of life.

Catherine: She goes to dozens and dozens of drop boxes in the course of these two elections.

Dinesh: Who's next?

Gregg: We call this one Backpack. So this guy approaches. What you're going to see is he approaches the drop box on his bike. He also has a backpack on. So he drives past the drop box, he comes over. He pulls the ballots out of his backpack and he puts them in. But you also see him get sort of frustrated as he starts to leave, because guess what? At this point, they started requiring the mules apparently to take pictures of the stuffing of the ballots. It appears that's how they get paid.

So they take a picture. They stuff it in—they take a picture. Not a selfie, but a picture of the actual ballot going in. But this guy gets frustrated. So he actually has to park his bike, gets off, kneels down, and takes a picture of the drop box, so apparently he can get paid. This is actually one of our top ten mules.

Catherine: So if you were there just casting your own ballot, what reason in the world would you have to come back and take a picture of the box?

Gregg: Now I'll show you one that we call Dog Guy. Middle of the day—this is actually at a polling place. The people in line are waiting to go in and vote early. They're doing it the right way. So these people are all waiting in line, and as he puts the ballots in, or starts to put the ballots in the box—one of the guys that's next to him actually engages him in a conversation. And he takes a picture too. He's got gloves on.

Catherine: He grabs his bag.

Gregg: Grabs his bag where the ballots are. His dog's looking around. Okay, you've got some other people who are going to walk up. This lady doesn't care. Neither does she. But this guy, this next guy, cares. He's watching the whole thing. The guy looks up, talks to him.

Catherine: He's got the ballots under his arm already and now he's got the rest that he pulled out of the bag.

Gregg: And he's got to get his camera ready to take pictures as he puts them in there. Consider the brazenness of this. This is the middle of the day. There's people there watching you cheat. People that are doing it the right way.

Dinesh: But it's difficult for them to know what to do, except observe and maybe say, what's going on here? What did I just see?

Catherine: But they carry that with them, don't they? They carry that view with them and they wonder, what does this all even mean, if it's happening in broad daylight and nobody's doing anything to stop it?

Gregg: And so these are the kinds of things—four million minutes of this. And it goes over and over and over again.

Dinesh: One of the slogans of the Democrats through all this debate has been "Make Every Vote Count." And I think we can now see, in a chilling way, that this is what they mean. What they mean is, it doesn't matter if all kinds of illegal ballots are being dropped in. Let's just count them. Make every vote count. There's no effort to qualify that by saying make every legitimate vote count. Or make every legal vote count. It's make every vote count, so that every vote that we can drum up with every which way, paid for or not paid for, legal or illegal—can neverthe-less go into the pile and end up making a difference.

Catherine: The ends justify the means.

·🎥

I thought it would be interesting to take Catherine and Gregg to California and have them show these videos to my fellow podcast and radio hosts at Salem Media. We convened a nice group: Charlie Kirk, Dennis Prager, Larry Elder, Sebastian Gorka, and Eric Metaxas. (Hugh Hewitt and Mike Gallagher declined to participate.) I'm including sections from the dialogue here because they show others reacting to the videos, some natural questions that arise, and the group's assessment of the significance of the geotracking and video evidence taken together.

Catherine: This one is Steelers—as you can see, she has a Steeler T-shirt on.

Charlie Kirk: Is this in Pennsylvania?

Catherine: This is in Georgia. She lives in South Carolina. You can't make this up.

Charlie Kirk: That doesn't make any sense.

Catherine: She's a bartender in South Carolina. This is 1:00 in the morning on January the fifth.

Eric Metaxas: But don't we all vote at 1:00 in the morning?

Catherine: Notice her countenance. Notice her . . .

Sebastian Gorka: Certitude.

Catherine: Her certitude.

Dinesh: Pause for a second. This seems silly, but somebody asked me, how do we know this is not normal mail? This is a ballot drop box. This is not the U.S. Post Office mailbox you use when you send a letter to your mom.

Sebastian Gorka: She's got gloves on.

Eric Metaxas: And what does she do with her gloves? Whoopsie-daisy.

Gregg: She's gonna take them off.

Charlie Kirk: Like she's making meth.

Gregg: And put them in a trash can that she never looked at when she walked up.

Eric Metaxas: She just happened to know it was there. You gotta show that again. It's hilarious. Look, look.

Sebastian Gorka: So this is not the first time she's done this.

Catherine: No.

Eric Metaxas: Eyes in the back of her head.

Sebastian Gorka: Wearing surgical gloves.

Catherine: And then dumping them.

Eric Metaxas: One move.

Charlie Kirk: In Georgia, it's illegal to turn in anyone but your own and your family member's ballot. So that's an illegal practice, what you just saw.

Catherine: And this is the guy we call Multiple. This is an example of multiple ballots.

Charlie Kirk: What time? It says 3 . . . 3:57 a.m.

Dennis Prager: Prime voting time.

Gregg: And this is one of our top ten.

Charlie Kirk: That's when I'm my most alert.

Larry Elder: Gotta beat the lines.

Eric Metaxas: I just want to repeat, 3:57 a.m.

Larry Elder: No gloves, I don't think.

Eric Metaxas: He needs a shoehorn.

Catherine: And we have lots of those, where they're just jamming them in and they fall on the ground because there's too many.

Dennis Prager: Well, this alone is, to say the least, suggestive. Who's voting at 3:57 a.m. with a whole bunch of ballots?

Gregg: And then to be able to match that ping, where he's standing alone, to the next place he goes, and the next place he goes.

Eric Metaxas: How many drop boxes?

Charlie Kirk: It's up on the chart. Twenty-four visits.

Eric Metaxas: So we're seeing a video of one of those.

Catherine: Right.

Larry Elder: Do you have video of the same guy going different places?

Catherine: Yes.

Charlie Kirk: Which is totally illegal.

Eric Metaxas: Can you say who some of the NGOs are?

Catherine: The circles you see—those are the NGOs.

Charlie Kirk: So the mules are getting the ballots from the organizations?

Catherine: Correct.

Dennis Prager: I do a heroic thing—I read the *New York Times* every day.

Eric Metaxas: That's crazy!

Dennis Prager: It's my martyrdom. So they claim, what is the Right talking about? In all these places we have found maybe four, maybe fifty, phony ballots. And these conservatives are talking about hundreds of thousands. So where does the *Times* get its figures from?

Gregg: They just make it up.

Dennis Prager: They just make it up?

Gregg: Absolutely.

Larry Elder: And these ballots aren't phony.

Catherine: These aren't phony ballots.

Dennis Prager: They're phony names?

Charlie Kirk: No.

Sebastian Gorka: There's no name on the ballot, Dennis.

Dennis Prager: Okay, wait. So let's say we got access to every single ballot? Would we be able to prove this is fraud?

Sebastian Gorka: It's the perfect crime, because the evidence cannot be curated after it's committed, because the evidence has no connection to the person who was meant to be voting. As soon as the ballot goes into the drop box, as soon as it's taken out of the envelope, the identity of the voter disappears.

Dennis Prager: The vote from John Doe is from a John Doe who is dead or a John Doe who has moved, correct? Why is that not provable?

Dinesh: It is provable. There's an easy way to bust it, but it's not the way you think. It's not to go find the ballots in the ballot mix. You can't do that. The way to find it is these guys, Catherine and Gregg, have the cellphone IDs of all the mules. All of them. So law enforcement has to step in at this point, and their next step is to go interview the mules. "Who paid you?"

Dennis Prager: Will any state's law enforcement do this?

Dinesh: This is a big question. The mules aren't going to 'fess up, of course. They know they are participating in something that's fishy.

Larry Elder: You've got them on videotape. You've got the evidence. They're not going to admit it.

Charlie Kirk: You indict five of these guys, light them up to the sun, and then they start to sing. That's how you take down the mob. Get the bag men, and they will point you to the heads of the crime families.

I'd like to conclude this chapter by laying out how the Salem panel evaluated the evidence they saw. I'll be making my own assessments and showing how this criminal operation must be dealt with, but that will come after my chapters further elaborating the scheme and establishing the infrastructure that the Democrats put into place to enable the coordinated ring of illegal vote trafficking. Here, then, are the provisional judgments of a group of intelligent commentators upon surveying the geotracking and video evidence presented by True the Vote.

Dinesh: Okay, guys, you've heard it. You've seen the evidence. What do you think?

Larry Elder: Republicans had no clue this was going on.

Charlie Kirk: Trump, to his credit, tweeted out in July, mail-in ballots are a disaster, and he was attacked so hard by Kemp and Ducey and so many other people.

Larry Elder: But he didn't have this information, obviously.

Charlie Kirk: His instinct ended up being right.

Larry Elder: But I mean, Republicans had no idea this was going on during the election.

Eric Metaxas: You're talking about extraordinary criminal activity.

Sebastian Gorka: What is the fraction of the election you covered? Did you cover 10 percent of the election? I've done the math, and you're talking about 2 or 300,000 ballots in only a few geolocations. But you're talking about, what, 5 percent of America?

Gregg: Less.

Sebastian Gorka: Less than 5 percent, okay. So case closed. Sorry gentlemen, lady, case closed.

Charlie Kirk: It looks pretty convincing to me. I don't think we'll ever know the full story, and what makes this crime so compelling and unique is that once the ballot enters the system it's really hard to reverse engineer. But when you have the geolocation data and then the actual footage of them doing what you expect them to be doing, taking pictures of the ballots, taking gloves off, visiting multiple times, I mean, it seems pretty clear to me. I've seen enough. And forget the Trump part of it, the control of the U.S. Senate went through Georgia with a tiny margin of votes. So Chuck Schumer is majority leader probably because of what we just saw.

Sebastian Gorka: What do we have empirically? We have data geolocated; we have footage of people harvesting ballots. Do we know who those ballots are for? We can't know who they were for. However, you have to inject common sense. Are we saying that in the centers of Democrat-held districts we are seeing hundreds and hundreds of visits to drop boxes with Trump ballots? It beggars belief. The election was stolen, and I don't need to have spurious theories about computers and foreign agents. If you look at the tradition of these cities, what do we know about them for fifty, sixty, seventy years? They are centers of left-wing voter fraud. This time we had the perfect storm. When you mail out tens of millions of ballots it's the equivalent of taking the contents of the bank and putting the bullion and the cash in the middle of the street. That's what happened.

Eric Metaxas: I'm sickened. I'm basically almost speechless. The level of cynicism involved in this vast criminal enterprise is to my mind demonic. There's a contempt for Americans, people like my old mother and father who voted, that's un-American and horrifying. I know most Americans will be absolutely sickened by this. They're not as cynical as the ruling classes that chatter on TV and write their columns. So I'm happy you're making this film, because you're telling them they're not crazy. That which they have suspected is in fact happening.

Dennis Prager: People know I'm crazy about telling the truth. If our guy won and there were serious accusations of cheating, I would want to clear my guy's name. That would be a moral sense, and even an enlightened selfishness on my part. You think our guy got elected unfairly, let's show you that didn't happen. So it's not a good sign that one side doesn't want any investigation. For their own sake, they should want it.

Number two, I voted for Donald Trump with passion, but I root for his having been defeated honestly. I'd rather lose honestly than have this come out as the way in which we lost. I love my country more than I want to win a debate. But if what—number three—if what you've shown is true, and the video is pretty powerful. I came in as an agnostic because my whole basis of saying I have any doubts about the legitimacy of the election was that there were too many anomalies. But I wasn't prepared to say—that's what an agnostic is, you're not prepared to say. What you showed is frightening. I'd like to hear the other side's answer to all this.

Charlie Kirk: They have two ways they'll try to invalidate it. One is minimizing and then slander.

Sebastian Gorka: Yeah.

Charlie Kirk: So they'll try to slander Dinesh personally, they'll say, "Oh, Trump pardoned him," or whatever and therefore he's trying to pay Trump back and reinforce the big lie. I can already see the headline in the *Washington Post,* "Trump-Pardoned Ally Comes Out with Questionable Movie."

Then they'll minimize it. They'll say it was only this and only that at the fringes. Then the third thing they do is to go to arguments from authority. I read the *New York Times* too. Not as much as you do, Dennis. They'll say "DOD, FBI, the intelligence community all unanimously say this was the most secure election." And so to an untrained eye, they'll say, "Well, if all those agencies say that, then how could it be wrong?" So slander, minimization, arguments from authority.

Sebastian Gorka: One more, I predict right now they'll say, "What on earth is a conservative doing tracking private citizens? What is Dinesh D'Souza doing to voters?"

Charlie Kirk: Invasion of privacy.

Sebastian Gorka: At 3:00 a.m. and that will be part of it.

Charlie Kirk: Intimidation will be the word. They'll say no person is safe. Communities of color are being tracked. People in black neighborhoods are now going to have to fear for their life that their cellphone pings will be paired. And this is Jim Crow 2.0, Dinesh, is what it is.

Sebastian Gorka: Dinesh, get ready.

Larry Elder: I disagree with everybody that this is not going to be compelling enough. This is a smoking gun. This is jaw-dropping. This is O. J. Simpson being seen leaving the scene of the crime. I don't care how partisan you are, you can't dismiss all of this. You can dismiss some of it. How do you explain somebody going to a whole bunch of different drop boxes with a whole bunch of different ballots on the same night at 3:57 in the morning? How are you going to explain that? I'm sorry, I think a whole bunch of people in this country are going to go, "Oh my God." And as for the leaders in both parties, they're going to have to come to grips with this.

Charlie Kirk: This is an Overton window moment. So documentaries can do this every once in a while. Michael Moore did it. He moved the Overton window on many different topics many years ago. Al Gore did it with climate change. This project, 2000 *Mules*, will move the Overton window generally on how we view voting, especially in urban areas.

The Overton window is the spectrum of how we view ideas in modern society. It goes from things that are unacceptable and unthinkable to policy. We all live the Overton window every day. Twenty years ago, you would have thought the idea of a transgender swimmer competing against women would be unthinkable. Now it's policy at the University of Pennsylvania. Defund the police went from something that was unthinkable to policy.

The same thing is going to happen, I believe, because of *2000 Mules*. It will happen, as Ernest Hemingway said, gradually and then suddenly, because it's not just how many people are going to watch the film. It's going to be lawmakers. It's going to be people that work for the Bureau. It's going to be someone somewhere with a conscience that has power and says, "This is a problem."

Larry Elder: It can't be dismissed.

Charlie Kirk: And it won't be.

CHAPTER 6

An Old-School Heist

I t seems at this point that our case has been proved. There was a heist of the 2020 presidential election and of the Georgia runoff elections. It was done on behalf of Joe Biden and the Democrats. What we don't yet know, however, is what enabled the heist. How, for example, did we get privately funded drop boxes for mail-in ballots? Who created the coordinated network of nonprofits that acted as vote "stash houses"? Who paid for it? And most specifically, where did the nonprofits get the ballots that they turned over to the mules for collection and delivery?

In the next two chapters, I will answer these questions. Here I focus on the last one, namely, how the nonprofits could have obtained the ballots. I say "could have" instead of "did" because there is only one way to know how each particular nonprofit got a hold of its ballots—that is, for law enforcement to arrest the mules and get them to talk. "Who asked you to do this? Who paid you?" The next step is to indict the activists in the nonprofits and get them to talk. "Who organized this? How did you get those ballots?"

I wish I could do this myself on behalf of law enforcement, but I can't. I have to rely on the authorities to do their job. What I can do, however, is reveal several ways in which activists working in nonprofit organizations can and have obtained ballots for the purposes of vote trafficking. It's an old-school heist that these groups have been perfecting on behalf of the Democratic Party for decades, actually for more than a century. Remember, we don't have to prove a heist here. We know there was a heist. We've tracked it; we've seen it. We simply have to show what could have happened behind the scenes to enable the heist.

In the previous chapter, Dennis Prager raised an interesting question: Why can't the illegal ballots be separated out from the legal ones? Behind this is a deeper question: Are the ballots being trafficked by the 2,000 mules genuine or fake? In other words, are they legitimate ballots from qualified voters that the mules merely deliver unlawfully to the drop boxes, or are they fraudulent ballots that do not represent the legitimate choices of voters and are somehow illicitly obtained and filled out by someone else?

You might expect me to say it's the latter, but the truth is actually more complicated. It's true that there is virtually no way for legitimate ballots, lawfully cast, to end up with mules. At the same time, these ballots we have been discussing are, for the most part, legitimate, as opposed to fake or counterfeit ballots. (There are some exceptions.) In many cases, the voters are also qualified, by which I mean they are eligible to vote. (Again, this is sometimes not the case.) Yet in general the fraud takes the form of legitimate ballots from qualified voters that are filled out by paid professional activists casting illegal votes in the names of those qualified voters.

To understand how this can happen, and does happen, and has frequently formed the basis for voter fraud cases in the past, we need to delve a little more deeply into the absentee ballot process.

Prager was confused that the fraud perpetrated by the mules could not be busted by retrieving the illegal ballots. But this presumes that there are voters' names on the ballots themselves. This is not the case. The ballot itself is marked with the choices of some candidates over others—for example, a check mark for Biden over Trump, or for Warnock over Loeffler—but the signature appears only on the outer envelope containing the ballot.

The absentee ballot process begins, in most cases, with a request or application for a ballot. In a few states—California, Colorado, Oregon, and Hawaii—absentee ballots are mailed out en masse without any requests from voters. But this is not typical and does not apply to the five states we are considering here. In four of our five states—Georgia, Arizona, Michigan, and Wisconsin—any voter can request an absentee ballot. In Pennsylvania, however, voters must have a legitimate excuse, such as being in a nursing home or resident care facility, to do so.

Absentee ballot applications are supposed to come from the voters themselves, and are submitted through request forms that must be signed by these voters. Yet these rules are not always complied with; in Michigan, Democratic secretary of state Jocelyn Benson mailed out thousands of unsolicited absentee ballot applications under the pretext that the Covid pandemic justified her actions, even though there was no warrant to do this under state law.[1]

When the ballot applications arrive, election officials check the voters' names against the voter rolls and then mail them the actual ballots, along with return envelopes. Voters must sign the return envelopes, attesting they are eligible to vote and that the signatures are in fact theirs. The filled-out ballots, which themselves contain no signatures, are then sealed in the envelopes and returned in person or by mail to be processed and counted.

Election officials are supposed to match or verify these signatures before counting the ballots, although as we will see this is not done with the necessary meticulousness or rigor. Consequently, the rejection rate for mail-in ballots in 2020 was extremely low compared with previous elections. This does not mean voters became more diligent; rather, it means that election officials became more lackadaisical.

But why? Not because election officials are incompetent. Rather, they were instructed not to be too diligent in checking signatures. In Michigan, the notorious Jocelyn Benson issued a directive that signatures should be presumed to be valid. Small deviations in signatures should be overlooked. Doubts should be resolved in favor of inclusion, not exclusion. Go ahead and discard the envelope and count the ballot! And once the ballots are detached from the envelopes, they disappear into the general pile and cannot be separated out again. The Benson directive was ruled invalid by a judge in early 2021, but

that ruling came too late to affect the 2020 election.[2]

To walk us through how election fraud of the kind we have been describing here can and does happen, let me introduce Hans von Spakovsky, a former commissioner at the Federal Election Commission and a fellow at the Heritage Foundation who is an expert on this topic. Hans, along with John Fund, is the author of *Our Broken*

Elections, an authoritative book on election fraud.

Dinesh: Hans, you just watched some mule videos and also the video with the mule 'fessing up about participating in a coordinated trafficking operation. You're an expert on the topic. Is this kind of a mule operation something familiar to you?

Hans: It is. And unfortunately it doesn't surprise me. We're talking about mules collecting these ballots, but unfortunately this is so common in some parts of America—particularly the Hispanic community—that they have a special name there. There they call them *politiqueros*. These are individuals paid by campaigns or political parties to go into neighborhoods and collect absentee ballots—to pressure and coerce voters to vote a particular way, oftentimes actually filling out the ballot for the voter.

Dinesh: Now people who observe election fraud have commented—even courts have commented—that absentee ballot fraud or mail ballot fraud is the most common type of fraud. Why is that?

Hans: Well, because they're the only kind of ballot that is voted outside the supervision of election officials and outside the observation of poll watchers. Transparency, as you know, is very important in the election process, and so there's no one there at a voter's home to observe what's happening. Also remember when you're in a polling place, you fill out your ballot and then you deposit it directly into the ballot box. That's obviously not what happens with absentee ballots.

If you hand them over to some stranger at your door, you have no idea whether they're going to deliver it—whether they might open it up and change it. If you stick it in the mail, again, you don't know if it's going to be delivered. You don't know if perhaps it will get stolen out of your mailbox and, again, changed or discarded.

Dinesh: There are some states that allow voter harvesting. And by voter harvesting, what we mean is you're allowed to give your ballot to someone else and ask them to deliver it. Now, are there any states in which you're allowed to pay a mule to deliver ballots to drop boxes?

Hans: No. You're not supposed to be doing that. Because you're giving third-party strangers, candidates, campaign staffers, party activists—all people who have a stake in the outcome of the election—you're giving them the ability to handle something very valuable, a ballot.

Dinesh: Let alone, if money is changing hands, doesn't it also violate the idea that this should not be a bribery operation? You should not pay people to participate in elections. It's something one should do out of a duty of citizenship, right?

Hans: That's exactly right. There's even an old term for this. They call it "walking-around money," which is money that candidates and others may give to particular individuals in certain communities to use that cash to either pay voters or to use it to collect individuals' ballots. And again, we don't really know what changes or alterations may be made to those ballots when these individuals get a hold of them.

Dinesh: Now we've shown that you've got these mules who are picking up these ballots at various—let's call them—vote stash houses. These could be nonprofits, they could be NGOs, they could be shelters. What I want to find out is, where could they conceivably have gotten those ballots?

Hans: Well, to quote Shakespeare, let me count the ways. There are so many different methods for doing this that we've seen in prior cases. Everything from filling out absentee ballot request forms for voters but having the ballot sent to them, to actually going to the voters and obtaining the ballots from them, to stealing them out of mailboxes, to actually using high-quality photocopy machines to make their own ballots.

Dinesh: Is it possible to get your hands on a ballot, make five hundred copies of that ballot, and then go to the voter rolls and look to find people who haven't voted lately, and use those copies to fill out those ballots yourself? If no one is carefully checking signatures, could you get away with that?

Hans: Yes.

Dinesh: How?

Hans: Voter rolls are in notoriously bad shape. States do a very bad job of taking people off who are no longer eligible to vote because they died or because they moved away. And it's very easy to get hold of a state's voter registration list and voter histories, and to figure that out. So if somebody's on the list and hasn't voted in ten years, you're probably pretty safe in trying to cast a ballot on their behalf, right?

And look, even when states are doing signature comparison, that's a very inexact art. Not even a science. And when an election clerk is looking at absentee ballots come in, they're looking at thousands of them. The average amount of time they have to quickly look at the signature on the ballot, the one on file, is a couple of seconds. So it's a fairly good chance that even if you're faking a signature, you're probably going to get away with it. And if they're not doing signature comparison, then it's really easy.

Dinesh: And isn't it true that in 2020 there were people like Jocelyn Benson who specifically instructed election vote counters to presume that signatures were valid unless there were multiple egregious discrepancies? So the benefit of the doubt goes to, yeah, let's get this vote through.

Hans: That's exactly right. Plus, remember the states that made the mistake of simply mailing out an absentee ballot to every single registered voter? Well, if you're a fraudster and you get a hold of that absentee ballot, you've got 90 percent of the information you need to fill it out. Because who are they going to mail the absentee ballot to? The person, the registered voter, exactly as they're registered. The name is going to be on the outer envelope, and also the registered address. So you've got most of the information you already need to cast a fraudulent absentee ballot.

Dinesh: Let's follow the track of these mailed out ballots, right? Let's just say you've got students on a campus; they voted in an election. But then they graduate and move to a different state, they go to a new job. If they're on the voter rolls, is it not a fact that their mail ballots will arrive in the dorms, and presumably they're not going to be hard to scoop up, if somebody knows when and where to look for them?

Hans: Exactly right. I work in the District of Columbia. They mailed out absentee ballots to all registered voters, and I can't tell you how many phone calls I got from people saying not only had their ballot arrived in the mail, but also other ballots—five, six, seven ballots all coming to their apartment for people who used to live there.

Dinesh: In your book you talk about the fact that prior to the 2020 election, a slew of lawsuits—you say four hundred or so lawsuits, the vast majority of them coming from the Left and from Democrats—were filed. What were those lawsuits aimed at doing?

Hans: Basically, getting rid of all the safety and security protocols that apply to the balloting process and to force as many states as possible to go to all-mail elections. They sued the state of Alabama saying that it should not be able to enforce their witness signature requirement. Many states have a requirement that when you fill out your absentee ballot you also have to have a witness sign it. That's one of the few ways to ensure that it really was the voter that filled it out.

Yet, because of Covid, the lawsuit said, Alabama shouldn't be able to enforce that requirement. Now fortunately, they lost. But there were other states where they were successful in that lawsuit. They filed a similar lawsuit in South Carolina, again trying to get rid of the witness signature requirement. In Alabama, they also wanted to get rid of the ID requirement.

Dinesh: Would it be fair to say that Republicans seem to have been taken by surprise and were not very effective in countering these lawsuits, as a result of which many of these processes were changed?

Hans: Well, in some cases they were too little too late, in part because of what I call collusive lawsuits.

Dinesh: What do you mean by that?

Hans: A liberal group sues a friendly liberal politician that's on their side. And that official, rather than defending the lawsuit—rather than defending the law—says, "Oh, I surrender. I'll settle. What do you want to do?" And that was the way they were able to waive and get rid of many state law requirements.

Dinesh: Which are some of the states where that actually happened?

Hans: North Carolina. That also happened in Pennsylvania, where state law says absentee ballots had to be in by the end of Election Day. Which makes perfect sense. Instead, the Democratic activists said, "Oh no. You're going to have to count absentee ballots coming in for three days after Election Day." And they were successful in that.

Dinesh: Now a former state supreme court justice in Wisconsin, Michael Gableman, has done a report on the election practices in that state. He points out that under Wisconsin state law, mail-in ballots are not allowed. At least, they're not allowed except under very limited conditions. Yet he says that disregarding this and in violation of the law, a number of these cities in Wisconsin took Zuckerberg money, and part of the condition of taking that money was to establish mail-in drop boxes, and so they just went ahead and did that.

Hans: That was a problem not just in Wisconsin but in other states too. Election officials and others simply said, "We're just not going to comply with the law. We're going to count ballots coming in even though they don't comply with state law requirements."

Dinesh: Gableman also points out there are approximately ninety thousand people in Wisconsin that are in resident care facilities or nursing homes. He plays videos of people who are clearly physically and mentally incapacitated—virtually comatose, don't know their names, don't know what year it is—and yet it turns out they voted. How could they have voted? What happened there?

Hans: This was a problem in Wisconsin in 2020, but it's a perennial problem and in many states. What happens is you have staff in those nursing homes, and some of them are political activists. What do they do? They get these individuals registered to vote. Or if they're already registered to vote, they request absentee ballots in their name, sometimes forging their signatures and then filling out the ballots for them.

Dinesh: We're identifying these problem areas. Campuses. Nursing homes. What about homeless shelters? You've got these places—shelters, soup kitchens—where you've got a population of homeless guys. And I'm guessing that probably a bunch of them don't even care about voting. Wouldn't it be relatively easy to tell these guys as they come in, "Hey listen. Sign here. We'll request an absentee ballot. It will be delivered not to you, because you're homeless, but to the shelter. We then get the ballot. Let us handle it from here."

Hans: Look, if a homeless guy is mentally capable, he ought to be able to vote. If the only place he can list as a registered address is a homeless shelter, that's fine. But the problem there is that it's very easy for the homeless to be intimidated and coerced into thinking, well, I'm not going to get food, I'm not going to get shelter, unless I vote the way these individuals here are telling me to do. This was exactly the issue a few decades ago in Chicago in one of the Justice Department's largest election fraud cases it prosecuted.

One thing common to many of the absentee ballot fraud cases that I've seen, and that have been proven in court, is these fraudsters pick on the most vulnerable in our society. They go into poor neighborhoods. They pick on the elderly. They pick on people for whom English is not their first language. They pick on the homeless.

Dinesh: What you're saying is that the vote traffickers are not motivated by the desire to help the homeless people who might not otherwise vote to cast a ballot. Rather, it's a cynical effort to collect their ballots, vote on their behalf, and make sure your candidate wins, using their names and their registrations.

Hans: That's really true. I've talked before about how in Texas they're called *politiqueros*. And in Florida, they're *boleteros*. It's these individuals who are paid to go into neighborhoods and into people's homes, collect their ballots, and pressure or coerce them to vote a particular way, often filling out the ballot for them. And one of the reasons they want to do this is they can't do it in polling stations. Statutes prevent candidates and campaign staffers from engaging in politics inside a polling place or even close to a polling place. Unfortunately those statutes don't apply in people's homes. Plus there are no poll watchers there to catch them in what they are doing.

Dinesh: Taking a quick look at American history, both parties have engaged in election fraud, and no one would claim this is a unique property of one party or the other. But isn't it also a fact that Democrats have primarily been the party of voter fraud? I say this harkening back to Tammany Hall and the era of the Democratic bosses. The voter suppression of the Democrats in the early twentieth century—particularly of the black vote.

Hans: Mayor Daley in Chicago.

Dinesh: The very close Nixon-Kennedy race of 1960, which tipped over to Kennedy largely because of Texas and Cook County, Illinois. So this is a party—the Democrats—that are sort of experts at this.

Hans: Most of the cases I see are unfortunately the Democratic Party.

Dinesh: And is that historically or now also?

Hans: Historically and now also. And it's not always one party stealing from the other. Some of the fraud you see is Democrats stealing from other Democrats. We've seen that in a number of cases. For example, there was a big case in Indiana—a local mayor's race, a mayoral primary—and that case went all the way to the state supreme court, which found there had been massive absentee ballot fraud in the Democratic primary.

Dinesh: I read these days constantly in the media that election fraud could occur—you might have a dead voter over here, a guy who moved out of town over there—but those cases are extremely rare. They are so episodic, we don't need to worry too much about them. They don't have the ability to tip an election. Is this true?

Hans: No. Fraud happens often enough that elections get overturned. Just go back a few years ago to 2018 and a congressional race was overturned. We have a database at the Heritage Foundation that we started a couple of years ago. We only put absolutely proven cases in there. So this is where someone has been convicted in a court of law or a judge has ordered a new election. We're up to 1,350-odd cases. But that's just the tip of the iceberg. It's really hard to detect fraud if you don't have the tools in place to detect it. If you're a state like New York or California that doesn't require an ID, well how are you going to know if someone shows up to vote in someone else's name? You're not going to know.

Dinesh: I remember the Associated Press did a story shortly after the 2020 election saying, we're looking at every proven case of voter fraud to show you how much voter fraud there is. But this seems to me like saying, we're going to look at every drug conviction to tell you how many people use drugs in America. Obviously the number of convictions is a tiny fraction of the actual number of people using drugs, right?

Hans: Right. And there are very credible reports of other cases out there that election officials aren't interested in making public because I think they're embarrassed. It shows they didn't engage in the kind of competent behavior they should. Also a lot of DAs just won't follow up on those. I've had personal experience with that.

I was on a county election board in Virginia when we found several hundred non-citizens who had registered. Many of them had actually voted in elections in Virginia. We sent that information to the local Democratic DA. We also sent them to the Justice Department. These would have been easy cases to investigate and prosecute. Because either you're a citizen or you're not. Nothing was done by the feds; nothing was done by the county DA about a single one of those cases.

Dinesh: Now Democrats say the reason they're filing all these lawsuits—against voter ID and rigorous signature checking and cleaning up the voter rolls—is they're making it easy for people to vote. But isn't it also true that they're making it easy for people to cheat?

Hans: They are. And there's no reason for these changes, because it's easier to vote in this country than ever before. It's simple to register to vote. It's easy to vote at a polling place. Most states now have early voting. States like Georgia and Indiana have had voter ID—photo ID—laws in place for more than a decade, since 2008 in fact. And we've got more than a decade's worth of turnout data to show that not only did their turnout not go down—Georgia with the voter ID laws had record voter registration and record turnout.

Dinesh: It's quite interesting that they use the phrase "Make every vote count." There's a missing adjective there. It's not make every *legitimate* vote count, make every *legal* vote count. To me, make every vote count is similar to someone who in the middle of a counterfeit operation says, "Make every dollar count." This is a cheater's mantra, don't you think?

Hans: Yes, I agree with you.

In a Heritage Foundation report published a few months before the 2020 election, Hans von Spakovsky reviewed cases of election fraud involving absentee ballots and mail-in voting over the last three decades.[3] In 2019, for example, a city council candidate in Hoboken,

New Jersey, Frank Raia, was convicted of "orchestrating a widespread scheme" targeting and bribing low-income residents for their absentee ballots. Raia evidently concocted the scheme when changes in state law eased requirements for mail-in voting. Previously residents needed to provide a justification for why they couldn't make it to the polls in order to obtain absentee ballots.[4]

In 1993, the California Supreme Court overturned a school board election due to widespread fraud and "tampering" with absentee ballots. In effect, a local activist group, the Fresno chapter of the Black American Political Association of California (BAPAC), took over the voter registration and absentee balloting process. This group—which targeted thirteen school board seats—controlled how minority voters got their ballots, how they filled them out, and how they were returned.

The basic scheme—orchestrated by a fraudster named Frank Revis, who headed BAPAC's Voter Education Project—was to visit people at their homes and get them to sign a voter registration form and an absentee ballot request form. The catch? These forms were to be delivered not to the voters but rather to BAPAC. Voters were instructed to leave blank the section that asked for the address to which the absentee ballot should be sent.

BAPAC then took the forms to its headquarters and filled in the address for the Voting Education Project (run out of BAPAC headquarters). When BAPAC received the absentee ballots, BAPAC staff took them to the homes of voters, where voters were "encouraged to vote in the presence" of BAPAC vote harvesters, who then reviewed their votes and collected the completed ballots for delivery to election officials. When evidence was presented at trial of voters who said their signatures had been forged or that BAPAC staffers had told them whom they should vote for, and of other illegal practices, the state supreme court acted to overturn the election, ruling that the fraud was pervasive enough to have affected the outcome.[5]

In 1999, the *Miami Herald* won a Pulitzer Prize for exposing fraud in the 1997 mayoral election in Miami.[6] Incumbent Joe Carollo won a plurality of the vote, but he fell 155 votes short of winning a majority. Carollo won a majority of the in-person votes, but his challenger, Xavier Suarez, won a majority of the absentee ballots. Carollo's failure to win an outright majority produced a runoff, which Suarez won in large part because he got two-thirds of all the absentee votes cast in the election.

The *Miami Herald* revealed numerous instances of fraud on the part of Suarez allies and the Suarez campaign. A former welfare official who was a Suarez volunteer pressured elderly food stamp recipients to vote for Suarez. Homeless voters were bused to city hall to drop off their absentee ballots and after that taken to a back lot of a church, where they were paid $10 apiece for their votes by "a man with a wad of cash." Suarez supporters were recruited to sign as witnesses for fraudulent ballots, including ballots cast by dead people, felons ineligible to vote, and nonresidents of the city of Miami.

Interestingly, while the trial court ordered a new election due to the widespread fraud, the court of appeals overruled that decision and instead reinstated Carollo as mayor, since he had won a majority of the votes once the fraudulent ballots had been subtracted. The appeals court said it would not "encourage such fraud" by simply holding a new election. Rather, the candidate who deserved to win in the first place should be restored to his legitimate office.[7]

In upholding Indiana's new voter ID law in 2008, the U.S. Supreme Court specifically referred to the absentee ballot fraud that occurred in the 2003 mayoral primary in East Chicago, Indiana, as a clear case of proven fraud.[8] The incumbent mayor Robert Pastrick got fewer votes than his challenger George Pabey. But a decisive margin in absentee ballots gave the election to Pastrick by a small margin of 278 votes.

After a trial, however, which included hearing from 165 witnesses, the trial judge found that the mayor and his cronies had "perverted the absentee voting process and compromised the integrity and results of that election." Among the judge's findings were the payment of compensation and bribes to voters—mostly first-time voters, the poor, and those with limited English-speaking skills. Also, Pastrick supporters routinely completed ballot applications and even ballots to which voters merely affixed their signatures, and these ballots were then delivered to Pastrick's campaign headquarters, where they were photocopied before delivery to election officials. The Pastrick campaign also induced city employees "who simply did not reside in East Chicago" to vote.[9]

Finally, let's talk about a more recent case, the overturned 2018 congressional election in North Carolina. Our Heritage Foundation source, Hans von Spakovsky, writes about this race in his report, but it is also the subject of a very interesting book by Michael Graff and Nick Ochsner, *The Vote Collectors*. This was the race for the Ninth Congressional District, which spans eight counties along the state's southern border. When the votes were tallied on Election Day, the Republican candidate, Mark Harris, won a decisive majority of the absentee ballots and narrowly defeated the Democratic candidate, Dan McCready.

An investigation, however, revealed that Harris's victory had been contaminated by an illegal vote trafficking operation run by one of his paid operatives, McCrae Dowless, a convicted insurance fraudster. Graff and Ochsner say that Dowless got into politics to get even with the district attorney who prosecuted him.

Dowless went to work for a black activist group called the Bladen Improvement Association and learned from the group how to traffic votes for its preferred Democratic candidates. Later, however, Dowless got into a dispute with the group, broke away from it, and offered his consulting services to Republicans as an expert in getting out the vote.

Whether working for Democrats or Republicans, Dowless followed the same old Democratic playbook. He sent paid workers door-to-door, had citizens sign absentee ballot request forms (that Dowless and his team had already filled out), and then photocopied the forms so that he would have all their important information, including birth dates, social security numbers, driver's license numbers, and even voter signatures (so he could forge them).

Dowless and his team would then go to voters' homes after absentee ballots had been delivered. They would pressure the voters to back the Dowless slate of candidates or to sign the ballot envelopes and give the blank or incomplete ballots to Dowless and his crew. Dowless's stepdaughter testified before the election board that she had filled out blank or incomplete ballots for Mark Harris and other Republican candidates.

Dowless—just like our mules—was careful not to dump whole sheaves of ballots in a single place at a single time. Rather, he would deliver small batches of absentee ballots to the post office. He ensured that ballots were mailed from post offices geographically near the registered voter whose ballot was being cast. Dowless, in other words, operated with the stealth and effectiveness of a well-trained Democratic fraudster, even though his fraud in this case was for the other party.

In February 2019 Dowless was indicted by a Wake County grand jury on felony charges of election fraud. (He passed away in 2022 before his case was adjudicated.) The North Carolina State Board of Elections decided the fraud was widespread enough to call a new election. This time, Mark Harris decided not to run and another Republican candidate, Dan Bishop, ended up beating the Democrat, Dan McCready, to represent the Ninth District.

My conclusion, reviewing this assortment of cases involving different types of races in different parts of the country at different times, is that election fraud, while hardly typical, is not uncommon either. It happens, and more often when absentee ballots and mail-in drop boxes are involved. Graff and Ochsner themselves write that in Bladen County, Dowless was simply the rare criminal caught for doing what various groups and schemers had been doing in countless political races in that county spanning many decades.

When the system makes it easier to cheat, the cheaters take advantage of those opportunities. As for the ballots, there are a whole slew of ways in which they could have been rounded up by the nonprofits involved in the 2020 mule operation. What we do know is that, however they got them, the whole scheme is unlawful in all the five states under examination, and therefore all the votes cast in this way are unlawful and should not have been counted.

CHAPTER 7

Following the Money

To commit a crime of this magnitude, to steal an election, requires an organizational and financial infrastructure. So who organized this? Who paid for it? Was it a conspiracy? Or was it something else?

Just prior to the 2020 election, the *New York Post* broke the story of Hunter Biden's laptop. The story, which revealed Joe Biden's direct involvement in a giant payoff scheme involving China and other foreign countries, was damaging enough that it could have, by itself, cost Biden the presidency. Yet the story was completely suppressed in the national media. Digital media even suppressed circulation of the *New York Post* story. Only after the election—indeed only in 2022—did the *New York Times* finally acknowledge that the Hunter Biden laptop was authentic and the story based on it a legitimate one.

This raises an interesting question: How did thousands of reporters from hundreds of media organizations manage to suppress this story? Did they get on a massive conference call and all say to each other, "This one is really damaging to our guy. If we publish this, he's finished. Let's none of us go with this story." Of course

TRUMP

not. They didn't need to. Why? Because they were all on the same political side and they all knew the implications of the story. So, acting in coordination, they all decided to suppress it, and the effect was precisely the same as if they had directly conspired with each other to do so.

I believe a coordination theory fully accounts for the election fraud carried out in the five critical states using the 2,000-plus mules. Consequently, all I need to show is the various elements of the fraud: What accounts for the proliferation of drop boxes throughout these urban areas? Who organized the mass dissemination of mail-in ballots that were illicitly obtained and manipulated? And who funded the mule operation and the nonprofit organizations that deployed the mules? The various bad actors here could be coordinating with each other and working toward the same end even if they are not actively conspiring with each other.

Time magazine, however, has a different idea. According to Molly Ball, a left-wing reporter for *Time*, there *was* a conspiracy. *Time* published a cover story on February 4, 2021, titled "The Secret History of the Shadow Campaign That Saved the 2020 Election."[1] Throughout the article Ball writes about "saving," "protecting," and "fortifying" the election, but from what? From Trump colluding with Russia to rig the result? This hoax had already been widely discredited—even though the full involvement of the Clinton campaign in promulgating it had not been fully revealed—so it couldn't have been that.

From election fraud on the part of Republicans? No one even considered this a plausible threat. One has to read the *Time* article very carefully to see that its underlying premise is that an organized conspiracy was necessary to prevent Trump's reelection, or, in Ball's words, "Trump's assault on democracy." While disavowing that the conspiracy was aimed at guaranteeing a victory for Biden and the

Democrats, the article goes on to make clear that the only way to save, protect, and fortify democracy in this case was to assure a victory for Biden and the Democrats.

Ball begins by quoting Trump. "It was all very, very strange. Within days after the election, we witnessed an orchestrated effort to anoint the winner, even while many key states were still being counted." Ball then remarks, "In a way, Trump was right. There was a conspiracy unfolding behind the scenes. . . . This is the inside story of the conspiracy to save the 2020 election. . . . The participants want the secret history of the 2020 election told, even though it sounds like a paranoid fever dream—a well-funded cabal of powerful people, ranging across industries and ideologies, working together behind the scenes to influence perceptions, change rules and laws, steer media coverage and control the flow of information."

The actions of the conspirators, Ball continues, "touched every aspect of the election. They got states to change voting systems and laws and helped secure hundreds of millions in public and private funding. They fended off voter-suppression lawsuits, recruited armies of poll workers and got millions of people to vote by mail for the first time. They successfully pressured social media companies to take a harder line against disinformation and used data-driven strategies to fight viral smears. . . . After Election Day, they monitored every pressure point to ensure that Trump could not overturn the result. They were not rigging the election; they were fortifying it."

Ball's article is so artfully presented that each line has to be decoded. My first observation is that her conclusion—that this is not election rigging but rather election fortification—does not follow from the premises. When one side alters voting systems and laws in its favor, deploys huge amounts of public and private funding to achieve its objectives, recruits armies of poll workers from its own team, installs a new system of massive mail-in voting, works in tandem with digital platforms to censor the opposition's messaging on grounds of "misinformation," and then blocks efforts to review, audit, or even publicly question the election result, this seems much closer to election "rigging" than election "fortification."

The one thing that Ball never mentions—I get the impression it's the one thing she assiduously avoids—is illegal ballot trafficking. There are numerous references in the *Time* article to getting out the vote—sometimes abbreviated GOTV—and getting people to vote by mail for the first time. There are glowing tributes to GOTV organizations such as the Voter Participation Center and All Voting Is Local, ostensibly nonpartisan groups staffed by left-wing activists that seek to increase voter participation in Democratic areas.

Nowhere, however, do we read that "get out the vote" in the 2020 election became "get out the mules." Election fraud itself is treated as a non-issue. Concerns on the part of Trump or Republicans about voter fraud appear only in the context of "voter suppression." Thus rules that make it easy to cheat become, in Ball's inverted logic, a tool for fighting voter suppression and protecting democracy.

What's valuable about this article is not what Ball seeks to convey—in fact, it's the very opposite of what she seeks to convey. What Ball reveals is how the Democrats constructed an elaborate infrastructure to enable an election heist, even though there is no reference in the *Time* article to the heist itself. Evidently the Democrats and the media wanted to boast about how ingeniously and laboriously they rigged the election without actually admitting that they rigged the election. They only, of course, "fortified" it.

***

To introduce the topics of the Democrats' organizational chart and money flow in the 2020 election, I'd like to introduce Scott

Walter, who is president of the Capital Research Center in Washington, D.C. Scott and I go way back; we worked together at the American Enterprise Institute early in my career and also on *Crisis* magazine, which I at one time co-edited with Michael Novak. Capital Research Center has been doing indispensable work in tracing how Democrats infiltrated the election offices and how the Left funneled a giant fund of cash into the nonprofit sector to (wink-wink) "get out the vote" for Democrats. Here's my interview with Scott, a part of which was featured in the movie.

Dinesh: Scott, the work of Capital Research Center has been aimed at tracking how money flows into the election process.

Scott: Sure. People think of three rivers of money, really, that empty into the gulf of elections. The first one is the hard dollars. You write a check to a candidate. The second is soft money, or dark money. People make that sound really scary, but it's actually a very small amount of money really. And there's a third river that people tend to neglect, and that's the 501(c)(3) nonprofit money.

Now that sounds fancy, but C3s just mean the kind of charity that you get to take a tax deduction for. Could be your church or synagogue—Salvation Army, Goodwill—that kind of thing. But there's a subset of those that focus intensely on public policy and even on winning elections, although by law they're not allowed to do that. That river is enormous. In the 2018 cycle, the sizes of those three rivers, for the hard dollars, about $5 billion. For the soft or dark money, just $133 million. But for the C3s, the nonprofits, about $21 billion.

Dinesh: What do the IRS regulations say about the involvement of these nonprofits, these so-called 501(c)(3)s, in direct electioneering and promoting a particular party or candidate?

Scott: By law, these nonprofit charities are forbidden to directly intervene in elections in any way. Or to help a particular party or candidate. And not only does the IRS say they can't intentionally intervene in elections—help a candidate—but they can't even have that effect. The IRS is emphatic that you cannot intend or even have the effect of helping one party or candidate over the other.

Dinesh: Now let's talk about some of the key elements of this particular network we're focusing on. We have drop boxes. And most people would think they are funded by the states. In other words, the drop boxes in Georgia are funded by the state of Georgia. The drop boxes in Pennsylvania were put in by the state of Pennsylvania. But that's not entirely the case, is it?

Scott: In the 2020 election there was an unprecedented hundreds of millions of private dollars going into government election offices. This was shocking.

Dinesh: Now who is the primary funder of this operation?

Scott: The $470 million or so dollars were sent by Mark Zuckerberg and his wife, mainly using monies that they had already put into the Silicon Valley Community Foundation, itself a C3 charity. And then that money went to two C3s. Most of it went to the Center for Tech and Civic Life (CTCL). Other places that put in much smaller amounts—one entity that put in $25 million was, again, a C3 nonprofit that's part of the Arabella Advisors, which, as a total empire, in 2020 took in nearly $1.7 billion.

Dinesh: Is there any evidence that this operation had a partisan thrust or a partisan character?

Scott: There's a lot of evidence that there was partisanship in multiple ways in how this was all carried out. First of all, the Zuckerberg charity was reaching out to a few specific localities, namely big cities that were guaranteed to be overwhelmingly Democratic in their turnout. And they were, therefore, targeting the big money there.

And as we all know, big money rarely comes without strings attached. So in the case of the CTCL, you as a local election official can't get that nice money—and of course all government employees want more money for their offices—unless you first signed a contract with CTCL and it had the strings spelling out lots of things that they want you to do. One of the big ones, typically, especially in places like Philadelphia, is lots and lots of drop boxes. And also lots and lots of vote-by-mail.

Dinesh: Would it be an exaggeration to say that while Republicans in 2020—and this may be more broadly true—focused on the campaign, Democrats focused on the process of actually running the election?

Scott: Yeah. One thing we've seen for years is that the Democratic side of elections focuses intently on all the little rules and regulations and all the intricacies of the process. There's even a think tank, the Analyst Institute—virtually no one has heard of it, and it's for-profit, so it doesn't have to report anything publicly—and it focuses on nothing but how to get out the vote, get out the vote. Every little way to nudge things, little by little, in the direction of the Democratic Party. And this was started by the political director of the AFL-CIO, who has for two decades now been one of the great organizers of the Left.

Dinesh: Now there was a very interesting article in *Time* about the 2020 election that focused on this guy, am I right?

Scott: Yes, it was written by a very left-wing journalist, who had previously written a gushing biography of Nancy Pelosi. The article spells out what the author herself calls a "conspiracy" and a "cabal." She said it was to protect democracy, to fortify democracy, and the rest. And her article depicts Michael Podhorzer of the AFL-CIO organizing dozens and dozens of left-wing Democratic-aligned groups, unions, nonprofits, foundations, and more. And you're supposed to imagine that all of these intensely partisan people who are constantly meeting and planning and conspiring and creating a cabal—they were just thinking about protecting democracy, but apparently they never gave a thought to who was going to *win* the election.

Dinesh: Now the Zuckerberg money flowing through two organizations—were those organizations staffed by neutrals or partisan activists?

Scott: Both the C3 nonprofits that got the hundreds of millions of Zuck Bucks in 2020 were created and staffed by left-wing partisans. The one that got the majority of the money, CTCL, its members all came from a previous left-wing C4, which is to say a more political type of nonprofit, called the New Organizing Institute. It trained thousands of Democratic activists every year. And it was called by the *Washington Post* the "Hogwarts of digital wizardry."

Dinesh: Now one thing I find amazing is that, before the election, Trump predicted the Democrats were going to cheat. That they're going to use the pretext of Covid. They're going to rig the rules in their favor.

Scott: The two sides don't approach elections in the same way. The Democrats—and especially the ancillary nonprofit world that does so much to help Democrats—they understand that the rules, the process by which elections are conducted, is just critical, and they have for decades been paying enormous attention to that.

Dinesh: Quite apart from this Zuckerberg money, your organization Capital Research Center has uncovered a separate, secret stash of money. Talk about that.

Scott: In addition to the $470 million or so that went into the Zuck Buck operation, you also had in 2020 an additional $120 million, very secretive fund, and the group that was the hub for the whole thing was called the Voter Registration Project. We're virtually the only place that has ever reported on that. No coverage in the mainstream media.

The people who ran the Voter Registration Project were so keen to keep it secret that on their LinkedIn pages they don't even list the name of their employer. So the $120 million came from a variety of sources. It came from the Soros foundation, it came from the Swiss billionaire Hans Wyss's foundation. It came from Warren Buffett's foundation. It came from unions like the SEIU and other government-worker unions. It flowed through a variety of pass-throughs like the Silicon Valley Community Foundation and the Proteus Fund and the Wellspring Fund. These are all ways of cloaking the original sources of these monies.

Dinesh: Now when you talk about the Silicon Valley Foundation, you're talking about a foundation where Zuckerberg has put in money, Jack Dorsey of Twitter has put in money.

Scott: The Silicon Valley Community Foundation is the place where billionaires like Zuckerberg and Dorsey are able to put in billions of dollars and then that foundation sends it further into the network, but no one knows anymore, "Well, that was from Zuckerberg's account" or Jack Dorsey's account.

Dinesh: And you've created a chart that lays out this elaborate network so people can see how Byzantine it is.

Scott: We actually use something called I2, which is a very sophisticated social network software that's used by military intelligence and the CIA and the Treasury Department for money laundering investigations. And you end up with this huge spiderweb with all these different entities and money going in different directions. And persons related to one entity but also holding another role at a different entity. It's staggeringly complex.

Dinesh: Wasn't the Voter Registration Project lauded in the *Time* article?

Scott: Yes, they were lauded for fortifying democracy, which they evidently did by spending millions of dollars to get absentee ballots mailed out to select voters. This is the same Voter Registration Project, by the way, that has as its goal increasing, in eight target states, over two million voters who are overwhelmingly expected to vote for the Democratic Party.

Dinesh: Which states?

Scott: Arizona. Georgia. North Carolina. Nevada. New Mexico. Those are five of the eight.

Dinesh: So here we've got an operation of illegal vote trafficking. You've got thousands of mules. They're being paid to do this. What you're saying is there is more than enough money available to fund any such operation. In fact, this would be only one part of a much larger effort to control the election.

Scott: The groups on the Left that work to win elections for the Democratic Party had at least half a billion dollars outside the normal political channels. We're not talking about money to the Democratic National Committee or the Biden campaign. We're talking half a billion in nonprofit charitable funds flowing into efforts to register and get out the vote for Democrats.

•☞

Picking up on Scott's remarks—and backing them up with the studies conducted by the Capital Research Center and other sources—we can identify three distinct stashes of money that enabled the theft of the 2020 election. The first was the legal stash, mainly under the control of a Democratic operative named Marc Elias. This money was for the purpose of changing the rules and loosening the verification standards. The second was the election infiltration stash, mostly bankrolled by Mark Zuckerberg. This was to pay for mail-in drop boxes and to get left-wing operatives into state and local government election offices. The third was the secret stash, funded by a large group of well-heeled Democrats, giving nonprofits the means to orchestrate illicit mule operations and other fraud schemes.

Marc Elias was one of the prime authors of the Russia collusion hoax, which he conducted on behalf of Hillary Clinton. Elias hired Fusion GPS, the firm that produced the so-called Steele dossier, named after former British intelligence officer Christopher Steele. Basically, the Hillary campaign invented a false narrative that Trump was somehow a "Russian asset" beholden to Vladimir Putin and that Russia had colluded with the Trump campaign to put Trump into the White House in 2016. This narrative was then used by the FBI and the media for four years to undermine the legitimacy and effectiveness of Trump's presidency. Elias was one of the key players in orchestrating this Russia collusion hoax.

Elias might be an unscrupulous political hack, but he also knows the ins and outs of the law. In 2008 Elias worked with the Al Franken campaign to challenge the narrow victory of Norm Coleman in the U.S. Senate race in Minnesota. There were ten thousand or so absentee ballots cast in that race that had been rejected for one reason or another. The normal political approach is to challenge these ballots and have each of them reconsidered and some of them included as valid votes to produce an updated tally. Challengers typically do this in the hope—often far-fetched—that it will produce a different result than the initial count.

But Elias developed a new and ingenious strategy based on challenging only certain ballots—the ballots likely to yield Franken votes. But how could you guess which ballots those were? For this purpose, Elias assembled a team of "microtargeting" experts who ran each of these ballots through a database which used a complex mix of personal, demographic, and polling information. Equipped with this information, Franken's lawyers were able to identify the unopened envelopes most likely to benefit their candidate.

The Elias team gave each voter—each ballot—a score of 1 to 100, predicting the likelihood that this was a vote for Franken over Coleman. For instance, Elias's statisticians knew that ballots that had been challenged for residential address discrepancies leaned Democratic, while ballots that had witness signature problems leaned Republican. The Elias strategy was to fight to get the Democrat-leaning votes counted while ensuring the Republican-leaning votes remained uncounted.

It worked. Over a protracted 7-month recount struggle, Elias was able to turn a 477-vote deficit on election day into a 312-vote lead when Coleman's last court challenge finally ended in the summer of 2009. This gave the Democrats their sixtieth U.S. senator, providing Obama with a filibuster-proof majority. Without this majority, it is doubtful that Obamacare would have passed. Coleman later admitted that he lost the election not because he got fewer votes but because he had been out-lawyered by Elias and the Democrats.[2]

Elias and his firm, Perkins Coie, have represented dozens of U.S. senators, governors, representatives, and their campaigns. He represented the Democratic National Committee, the Democratic Senatorial Campaign Committee, the Democratic Congressional Campaign Committee, the National Democratic Redistricting Committee, and many left-wing political action committees. He has been paid more than $170 million by Democratic campaigns, committees, and candidates since 2009, not including fees paid by nonprofit and activist groups to attack and undermine voter ID laws.[3]

In the 2020 election alone, Elias took in more than $60 million. This was largely for the purpose of challenging election rules aimed at ensuring that only eligible voters can cast ballots. Elias had two primary objectives. The first was to prevent the cleaning up of voter rolls, ensuring that voters who had died or become incapacitated or moved, or ineligible persons such as felons or illegal aliens, would nevertheless remain on the rolls—creating promising opportunities for fraudsters to vote in their names.

Elias's second objective was to block the means for election officials to accurately validate ballots by checking IDs and matching signatures. Voter ID laws require voters who cast their ballots in person to produce valid IDs, and signature matching rules call for a careful comparison between the signature on record and the signature on the mail-in envelope. Elias filed innumerable lawsuits, together with other Democratic groups, alleging that these rules had a "disparate impact" on black and other minority voters, effectively "disenfranchising" them.

This argument is prima facie absurd. Those very same black and minority voters seem to have no trouble producing IDs when they open bank accounts, fly on airplanes, collect their government benefits, or do many other things that cannot be done without proper identification. Even so, Elias with a straight face contends that it is simply too much to expect that these individuals produce valid identification before casting a vote.

As for signature matching, once again Elias takes the view that rigorous comparison of signatures tends to result in more minority votes being rejected. This, he argues, is a form of voter suppression. Preposterous though these arguments are, Elias has had reasonable success with them, usually with secretaries of state who are Democrats or in courts with judges who are Democratic appointees.

Even Republicans tend to be intimidated when Elias and other Democrats invoke the specter of segregation and Jim Crow—even though Jim Crow laws were all passed by Democratic legislatures, signed by Democratic governors, enforced by Democratic officials, and have not been on the books for decades. Shamelessly invoking the bad old days of the past, Elias has also pushed to loosen legal restrictions on ballot trafficking, insisting that "community organizations" should be allowed to collect and harvest ballots on behalf of minority voters who are supposedly too timid, unsophisticated, or preoccupied to do this for themselves.[4]

In 2020, Elias and his allies exploited the Covid pandemic to change the election rules in many states. In some cases, states mailed absentee ballot applications, or even ballots, to every single name and address on their voter rolls. They flooded Democratic voting areas with ballot drop boxes and offered prepaid postage on election mail. Some states adopted signature-matching standards that had been diluted to the point that they were virtually inoperative.

As Mollie Hemingway summed up the outcome: "Alabama, Arkansas, California, Connecticut, Delaware, the District of Columbia, Georgia, Illinois, Iowa, Kentucky, Maryland, Massachusetts, Michigan, Minnesota, Missouri, Montana, Nebraska, Nevada, New Hampshire, New Jersey, New York, North Carolina, Ohio, Oklahoma, Pennsylvania, Rhode Island, South Carolina, Texas, Vermont, West Virginia, and Wisconsin all made changes to expand mail-in balloting. Arizona, Colorado, Florida, Oregon, and Washington already had widespread or universal mail-in balloting. It was a sea-change to the American electoral system, and Elias was the man responsible for much of it."[5]

‎·‎

Mark Zuckerberg, the founder and CEO of Facebook—now called Meta—is recognized as the man who funded many of the mail-in drop boxes. He did do that, but he did a lot more. Working through two obscure nonprofit organizations run and staffed by Democratic activists, the Center for Tech and Civic Life (CTCL) and the Center for Election Innovation and Research (CEIR), Zuckerberg funneled more than $400 million for the purpose of planting left-wing operatives into the nation's election administration system itself.

This was unprecedented, brazen, and, for the most part, perfectly legal. No one had anticipated that a private individual could infiltrate, and in some cases take over, the election administration of the states themselves. Consequently, in 2020 there were no laws against this. (There are now.) Yet the effect was to give Democrats a huge advantage—to tilt the playing field in their favor. In the words of Mollie Hemingway, "It was as if the Dallas Cowboys were paying the National Football League's referee staff and conducting all of their support operations."[6]

As Democratic legal operatives like Elias pushed for mail-in drop boxes across the country, but especially in the heavily Democratic precincts of swing states, the question naturally arose: Who will pay for those drop boxes? Zuckerberg, in effect, answered, "I will." His justification was that he was contributing to election integrity by making it easier for people to vote. What he didn't say is that he was also undermining election integrity by making it easier for Democrats to cheat.

Zuckerberg's two left-wing funding channels, CTCL and CEIR, didn't merely bankroll the drop boxes; they also used their financial leverage to pressure counties to install drop boxes. Basically, the Zuckerberg grants came with three conditions: more mail-in drop boxes; "voter education" focused on people from poor and historically disadvantaged communities, including non–English speaking voters; and involvement of an assortment of left-wing activist groups in these operations as well as the systems of election administration. In sum: you let us run your election for you and we will largely pay for it.

Without Zuckerberg's privately funded drop boxes, it's hard to see how Democrats could have conducted their illegal mule operation. It's not so easy to run this operation through the U.S. Post Office. Interestingly, CTCL's grant letter to Philadelphia specifies the need for electronic surveillance of drop boxes, and provides funding for this purpose.[7] Yet True the Vote has not been able to obtain drop box electronic surveillance video from Philadelphia, and it's not clear whether it's because they don't have it, or because they have it and won't provide it. Either way, what's the point of electronic surveillance when you can't look at the video to see what's going on?

CTCL and CEIR were obscure, small-time groups prior to the 2020 election. Then suddenly they were flush with hundreds of millions of dollars to disperse for drop boxes and election administration. Even so, they operated largely behind the scenes in these efforts, with very little media coverage of what they were doing. We heard a great deal from the media in 2020 about "dark money." Yet Zuckerberg's money was as dark as it comes, and the media showed little interest in investigating where it was going. Essentially the media was coordinating—not conspiring but coordinating—with Zuckerberg to enable his project to function without public awareness or scrutiny.

There were a few media reports on Zuckerberg's money—colloquially called Zuck Bucks—going into the election, but mostly the mainstream media made it appear that Zuckerberg was paying for Covid protection. This was a political diversion. "Look, the guy is just paying for masks." In reality, Zuckerberg was following the Democratic playbook in using Covid as a pretext to dramatically alter election operations, to take them over into what Judge Gableman has quite accurately described as an elaborate "bribery scheme."

Once the impact of the Zuckerberg infiltration became clear—and the *Wall Street Journal* and others took public note of it after the election—CTCL and CEIR representatives insisted with a straight face that they were strictly neutral and nonpartisan in the way that they awarded grants. They gave money to Democratic counties that went for Biden, and they also gave money to Republican counties that went for Trump. But the veil of nonpartisanship falls when we see how much money these groups gave to Democratic counties as opposed to Republican counties. Zuckerberg money, it turns out, was crucial in steering the swing states toward Biden and the Democrats.

Ten percent of the Zuckerberg funding went to Georgia—more than $30 million—with the money heavily concentrated in Democratic counties that received, on average, $7 per voter, while Republican counties received an average of less than $2 per voter.

Not surprisingly, counties that got very little or no Zuckerberg money showed hardly any change in partisan shift from the previous election in 2016, but counties flush with Zuck Bucks moved significantly toward Biden and the Democrats. This pattern continued after Election Day as Zuck Bucks flowed into the Georgia runoff election, with two-thirds of the allocation going to the Democratic counties of Fulton and DeKalb, to help boost the prospects of the two Democratic candidates running for the United States Senate, Jon Ossoff and the Reverend Raphael Warnock.

Mollie Hemingway writes, "Georgia's election results moved more than five points in the direction of the Democratic presidential candidate from 2016 to 2020, resulting not just in Trump's defeat but the capture by Democrats of two key Senate races." The Georgia mules were obviously a key part of this, providing a sufficient margin by themselves to tip the state, but Zuckerberg's funding bankrolled a whole Democratic get-out-the-vote operation in the state that went far beyond mules and mail-in drop boxes.

In Pennsylvania, Zuckerberg funding also had a measurable impact. According to Capital Research Center, more than 95 percent of the Pennsylvania-allocated Zuck Bucks were dedicated to ten counties, amounting to a combined $21 million. Biden won eight of those ten counties. The counties Biden won were more than three times more likely to get Zuck Bucks than counties Trump won. Trump counties got around 50 cents per capita, while Biden counties got almost $3. Philadelphia—the center of the Democrats' mule operation—got more than $6 per capita, compared to around $1 for the highest-funded Republican county.

Zuckerberg funding in Wisconsin was concentrated in five cities: Milwaukee, Madison, Racine, Green Bay, and Kenosha. Here we see Zuckerberg's election infiltration in all its perverse glory. The Center for Tech and Civic Life offered these cities a variety of "services," all aimed at influencing the election results. Basically, CTCL imported into the Wisconsin election process a plethora of left-wing organizations that became involved in virtually every aspect of the election, from designing the absentee ballots to overseeing the drop boxes, to get out the vote in these heavily Democratic areas of the state.

The Center for Civic Design, in partnership with a number of left-wing organizations, designed absentee ballots and voter instructions. The Elections Group, also linked to the Democratic network, conducted "voter outreach." Another left-wing advocacy group, the Center for Secure and Modern Elections, helped develop Spanish-language radio ads to target Hispanic voters in Green Bay. Power the Polls, a left-wing activist group, came to help with ballot curing—a process of correcting votes cast with missing or inaccurate information. Another left-wing group, the Mikva Challenge, recruited high-school-age poll workers. The progressive Brennan Center was on hand to assist with "post-election audits" and "cybersecurity."

In perhaps the most egregious example of Zuckerberg infiltration anywhere in the country, the Democratic mayor of Green Bay, Eric Genrich, invited Zuckerberg's operatives to virtually take over the election process: running and supervising voter outreach, collecting absentee ballots, correcting and fixing ballots that would otherwise be rejected for failing to conform with legal requirements, and even overseeing the counting of ballots. This is a clear violation of

Wisconsin law, which makes it a felony for anyone other than state election officials to manage these processes.

We now know from a series of emails that a Zuckerberg operative named Michael Spitzer-Rubenstein, a New York left-wing activist from a group called the National Vote at Home Institute, had keys to the central counting facility and access to the absentee ballots as well as the electronic machines before Election Night. He handled ballots. He told poll workers what to do. He was the contact person for the hotel hosting the ballot counting, and he ran the count operation on Election Night.

This out-of-state Democratic operative essentially pushed aside the Green Bay city clerk, Kris Teske, who was the lawful agent supposed to be doing all this. "I am being left out of the discussions and not listened to at meetings," Teske wrote on July 9, 2020, as the Democratic mayor Genrich and Spitzer-Rubenstein created a new team to oversee election operations that excluded Teske. Displaced and frustrated, Teske took a leave of absence just days before the election and resigned shortly thereafter.

＊＊

Now we turn to a secret nonprofit network, established by the Democrats, that received more than $120 million from leftist donors in the months leading up to the 2020 election. The ostensible purpose of this network? To "get out the vote." But these nonprofits were also where the mules picked up their fraudulent ballots.

Nonprofits are strictly forbidden from engaging in electioneering for the benefit of a particular party or candidate. "Under the Internal Revenue Code, all section 501(c)(3) organizations are absolutely prohibited from directly or indirectly participating in, or intervening in, any political campaign on behalf of or in opposition to any candidate for elective public office."[8]

Even so, in flagrant violation of these rules, a network of non-profits did engage in electioneering for the direct benefit of the Democratic Party. Quite apart from law enforcement's cracking down on the mules, the IRS must investigate and, if appropriate, withdraw the tax-exempt status of these groups and penalize them for their unlawful participation in the 2020 election.

According to the Capital Research Center, the money flowed through a nonprofit called the Voter Registration Project (VRP) for its so-called Everybody Votes Campaign. VRP is a secretive nonprofit that has stayed almost completely out of the public eye. It has no website and has apparently never been covered by any news organization.

Who funds VRP? It's the mega-donors of the Left and the Democratic Party. Since many of these figures are celebrities, it's even more curious that they have attracted no public attention. Two of the most high-profile donors are the Susan Thompson Buffett Foundation (the private foundation of Warren Buffett) and George Soros's Open Society Foundations.

Other billionaires, who strive to keep their names out of the public eye, also pitched in. Hedge fund manager C. Frederick Taylor gave money, along with his partners at the Wellspring Philanthropic Fund. So did the Wallace H. Coulter Foundation. VRP got $2 million from the Civic Participation Action Fund, which is financed by Chuck Feeney.

A plethora of left-wing foundations are also part of the action. The Proteus Fund gave $13.5 million; the New Venture Fund, $13 million; the Hopewell Fund, $7.8 million; with smaller grants in the $500,000 to $1 million category coming from the Tides Foundation, a group called Impact Assets, and NEO Philanthropy. These are all "dark money" groups on the Democratic left.

Labor and environmental groups also gave to VRP, including the Service Employees International Union (SEIU) and the American Federation of State, County, and Municipal Employees (AFSCME). VRP got just under $10 million from the League of Conservation Voters Education Fund and a smaller contribution from NextGen America, an environmental activist group funded by billionaire Tom Steyer.

Finally, VRP also got money from the Silicon Valley Community Foundation, which is a funnel for left-wing tech billionaires. Facebook creator Mark Zuckerberg, Twitter founder Jack Dorsey, Netflix cofounder Reed Hastings, and WhatsApp cofounder Brian Acton have all poured money into this foundation, which then makes grants on their behalf but without a direct connection to any of them. So quite apart from the direct intervention of the tech moguls in the 2020 election—by suppressing and manipulating content on their platforms—they also helped bankroll the Democrats' "get out the vote" campaign.

While VRP poses as a nonpartisan organization merely doing its civic duty and motivating Americans to get out and vote, the Capital Research Center has uncovered documents showing that it was operating through a specific plan, focused on key states such as Arizona, Florida, Ohio, Georgia, and North Carolina, to secure two million additional votes for the Democratic Party.[9]

This plan seems to have been originally devised in 2015 by a group called Corridor Partners, consultants hired by the private foundation of Swiss billionaire Hansjörg Wyss. The plan was offered to John Podesta, campaign manager for Hillary Clinton, for execution in the 2016 election. It didn't specifically refer to mules or any illegal operations. It did say, "The goal of this effort is to fundamentally change the composition of the electorate in a number of states."

The Everybody Votes Campaign of VRP, which was deployed in the 2020 election, seems to be directly lifted from the Corridor

Partners plan. Both have the same price tag: $105 million. Both refer to a five-year period of execution: 2015–2020. Both involve eight focus states, although VRP makes a couple of substitutions, trading out Illinois for Ohio and Virginia for New Mexico. Both aim to produce more than two million new voters by 2020—voters who are overwhelmingly expected to cast ballots for the Democratic Party.

Now how did VRP deploy its massive arsenal of funds in the 2020 campaign? Basically, it channeled the funds through a group called State Voices. This is a national group that oversees and coordinates a network of leftist organizations in the various states. In addition to bankrolling this umbrella group, VRP also gave directly to several of the state and local groups as well: Blueprint NC in North Carolina, ProGeorgia, Minnesota Voice, Pennsylvania Voice, and Wisconsin Voices. Sure enough, State Voices in its 2020 *Post Election Report* takes credit for adding 2.1 million voters in the 2020 election.

In addition, VRP gave $10.4 million to the Voter Participation Center, the group credited in *Time* magazine with sending mail-in ballot applications to fifteen million people in key states and getting nearly five million people to return them. Other beneficiaries include the League of Conservation Voters Education Fund, the Mi Familia Vota Education Fund, the Fair Share Education Fund, One Arizona, the Ohio Organizing Collaborative, and the New Virginia Majority Education Fund.

One can see from this setup that we are dealing with a secretive financial network that deploys its resources through foundations that in many cases camouflage the identity of the donors. These foundations then bankroll nonprofits, which in turn funnel money to other nonprofits, which in some cases channel the money to still other nonprofits. It's a dense menagerie populated by creatures who pose as neutrals but who have a common goal: to deliver elections to the Democratic Party.

I set out to show who could have funded the mule operation, and have shown that there is a giant cluster of heavily funded nonprofits that seem to be engaging in blatant partisan activity in clear violation of IRS guidelines. These groups helped change the rules of the 2020 election, in some cases infiltrated the election process itself, and ran giant operations ostensibly aimed at "making every vote count" but in fact ensuring a winning margin for their own preferred political party.

CHAPTER 8

Looking the Other Way

D espite all the anomalies of the 2020 presidential election, until True the Vote purchased the geotracking data and did the work, and then confirmed it with the video evidence it obtained from open records, no one could really *prove* beyond a reasonable doubt that the election was stolen. Nevertheless, can it really be true that no one in the Republican Party had any idea that the Democrats were trying to steal the election? Trump, let's remember, predicted that there would be massive voter fraud. He specifically referenced mail-in ballots. The obvious question is whether the Republican establishment took any steps to catch this fraud while it was happening.

To answer this question, let's turn to a conversation featured in the movie *2000 Mules* between investigative reporter Heather Mullins and a Georgia police officer who decided to become a whistleblower. The interview was conducted in Atlanta in mid-March 2022. The police officer asked that his identity be concealed, but he is obviously known to the people who hired him to provide election security, and he is willing to come forward and testify to what he did, saw, and recorded. I also reviewed his email communications and invoices to confirm his employment during the Georgia U.S. Senate runoff election. It all checked out.

Heather Mullins: How did you get involved—what was your role—during the 2020 election?

Police Officer: My role was to watch ballot boxes in my area. We had three—actually four, we had four ballot boxes. Two at a center and two others on a remote site. My job was basically to watch the ballot boxes. I was hired by the NRSC (National Republican Senatorial Committee). A gentleman by the name of John. I'll leave it at that. That was through an intermediate person who had made contact with me. John was a security guy that worked for NRSC. He asked if I could watch ballot boxes. And I said yeah, sure, no problem.

He said, "Well, this is what we're going to pay you," and I said, "Fine. Sounds good to me." He said your hours will be 8:00 a.m. to 8:00 p.m. This was for the early voting in Georgia, so that started on December 14. It ended on December 31. Then we would come back on the fifth, which would have been the runoff, the Senate runoff. The Georgia Senate runoff. And we would monitor the box from 8:00 to 8:00, all day long.

So consequently during those two weeks I monitored those boxes indiscriminately. I would move around to the different areas of the boxes and watch them—thirty minutes here, an hour there. And then I'd start to see things where I'd see people walking up with backpacks, and they were unloading large numbers of ballots, stuffing them into the box. I recorded some of that. Took pictures of it and dates and times and those things.

I also spotted a lot of vehicles that were coming from rural counties—not the area that we were in. I spotted plates from Texas, from Colorado, South Carolina, North Carolina, and I just thought that was odd that all these states were coming in, and these people would get out, and I would watch them get out, and they'd go up and stuff the ballots in the ballot box. I thought that was kind of odd.

So we took pictures of those things. Recorded license plates and those things. And then I uploaded those photographs to a drop box that I had to upload them to. So I did that for that amount of time and then when it came to the Georgia runoff—the actual day of the election, January 5—I was up there early in the morning. I had come up there, and it was really busy around the site, because a lot of people were coming in, a lot of people going out.

I noticed a gentleman was standing over there close to the door. He was probably about twenty feet away or so. I kind of watched him and kind of figured he was watching the ballot boxes, but I didn't know who he was. So I walked inside the building, and basically had some small talk with him, and he mentioned that he was working for the Georgia Republican Party. And I said, "Oh." And he said, "I'm kind of doing the same thing you're doing. Watching the ballot box." We stood there all day long.

About 6:30 that evening, we noticed there was a couple, female couple, light-skinned woman and another woman. They were running up to the box. Now there were Stacey Abrams people all along the sidewalk up there.

Heather Mullins: How did you know they were Stacey Abrams people?

Police Officer: Well, they had those masks on that said "VOTE." She has one of those things—this is during Covid, right? And they were part of that initiative. I knew she was part of that initiative that she had going on about get-out-the-vote kind of thing. So it was the Democratic Party and it was Abrams people—they were all inter- acting with each other. And the local Democratic Party chairman was there also, earlier in the day, and stayed right up until seven o'clock, when the voting had closed.

Heather Mullins: So this is January 5, Election Day for the runoffs.

Police Officer: January 5. The actual day of the runoff election. So these two ladies had run up, and they had a big stack of ballots. And we're standing there, and they tried to shove the ballots in there. I'm looking at it and the other gentleman took some video of everything. And she turned around and looked at us and I said, "Well, we're taking your picture." And she said, "You can't do that." And I said, "Yes I can." And she got mad. And she ran up the sidewalk and left.

And the other gentleman was like, "Yeah, I got it. Got it all on video. We're going to go ahead and forward that in." And I thought that was kind of odd, you know? "One ballot, one vote." But no, we've got people coming in with multiple—every day I see multiple ballots being stuffed in those boxes. Sometimes four, five, sometimes ten. Sometimes more.

Heather Mullins: What were you specifically instructed to do by the NRSC when you witnessed these kinds of activities?

Police Officer: So we would take a picture of it. Notice, write down the times, dates, and basically write down the information associated with it. Get anything, any more information we could and then we had a drop box that evening we'd upload it to. In the morning when I started my shift, I took a picture of the actual box I was monitoring, and in the evening when we were done. And that was proof that we were there. That was proof so they could pay me.

Heather Mullins: And you did get paid?

Police Officer: I did. I was paid.

Heather Mullins: So you're saying the NRSC was made aware that there were people stuffing drop boxes at specific dates and times?

Police Officer: Yes. And I thought somewhere down the line I'd be contacted by somebody—I'd have to do a deposition, you know, something legal and all that stuff. Nothing ever developed from it.

Heather Mullins: You're saying that if somebody had contacted you, you would be willing to testify to these things and give depositions under oath?

Police Officer: I would have had to. I would have had to.

Heather Mullins: So did you ever reach out to anyone, like when the NRSC did not get back to you?

Police Officer: I did. I sent several messages to them, and I also sent several messages to one of the Georgia representatives that were holding a hearing. I said, "Hey, ask this. What about this? What about that?" And it was totally ignored.

Heather Mullins: Why do you think it was ignored?

Police Officer: I don't, I don't know. It's hard to tell. But I pretty much, like I said—everything just, I didn't think of anything after that point. I was like, "Okay, it wasn't important to them." So it wasn't important to me anymore. Until all this stuff surfaced. Once it surfaced, now it's becoming a big deal.

Heather Mullins: So with what you witnessed during your time watching these drop boxes, do you believe there was enough for law enforcement to get involved?

Police Officer: Oh definitely. I mean knowing what I know about it, I would think that somebody would contact us and say, "Hey look, I'm an attorney. We need to do a deposition here. We need to investigate this thing." I thought it was important. But after several weeks, no contact or anything, I just didn't think anything of it anymore. It was done, it was over with. The election was done and—it's history.

*

To understand the peculiar response of the Republican leadership to election fraud, let's consider the behavior of two key figures, Georgia governor Brian Kemp and his secretary of state Brad

TRUMP

Raffensperger. Although there is no physical resemblance between the two, I call them the Zigzag Twins. That's because of their peculiar penchant for zigging one way and then zagging the other, so that their position on this issue becomes virtually impossible to figure out.

Initially, both Kemp and Raffensperger insisted that the 2020 election in Georgia had been free and fair. No problems whatsoever. When Trump made his now infamous phone call to Raffensperger asking him to "find" additional votes, Raffensperger pushed back—and leaked the audio of the call to the media. This is the call Democrats used in their second impeachment of Trump as part of their claim that he sought to subvert the results of the election.

For the media, Raffensperger became the poster boy of Republican virtue. He was supposedly one of the last honest Republicans, resisting bogus efforts to overturn the election results. Reveling in his new celebrity, Raffensperger appeared on *60 Minutes* in January 2021 and said, "We had safe, secure, honest elections."[1] Since Trump had been insisting nonstop that Georgia's election was anything but fair, Raffensperger's statement to the contrary was widely hailed by the media. He became Trump's public nemesis, and he had Governor Kemp as an ally.

Both Raffensperger and Kemp rebuffed a lawsuit filed by the Trump campaign and David Shafer, chairman of the Georgia Republican Party. "Our lawsuit does not rely on theories about the voting machines," Shafer said. "Instead, using official government data and licensed sources, we show thousands of examples of low-tech voting irregularities and fraud sufficient in scale to place the election result in doubt."

The suit accused Raffensperger of failing to maintain and update an accurate list of registered voters. It pointed out that poll workers who reported irregularities were fired in retaliation. It confirmed that Fulton County election officials had, notwithstanding their denials, shut down vote counting on Election Night, packed everything up, and then resumed when the observers and monitors had left.

The lawsuit alleged that more than 2,500 ineligible felons voted. More than 66,000 underage people were registered. Thousands of people voted who were not on the state's voter rolls. Thousands more registered in another state after they registered in Georgia, making them ineligible voters. More than 40,000 people moved counties without re-registering. More than 10,000 deceased people voted. More than 300,000 people applied for an absentee ballot past the deadline, which was 180 days before the election.

The lawsuit also compared data from the 2020 election to the elections in 2016 and 2018 to show that the state of Georgia had performed virtually no signature matching on absentee and mail-in ballots. In 2016, 2.9 percent of ballots were rejected; in 2018, 3.46 percent; in 2020, 0.34 percent. Indeed, 48 out of Georgia's 159 counties did not reject a single mail-in ballot in the 2020 election. Under conditions of normal scrutiny, this would be a statistical impossibility.

But conditions were not normal in the 2020 election. In March 2020, Raffensperger had signed a "Compromise Settlement Agreement" with the Democrats. This was in response to the submission by Stacey Abrams, Marc Elias, and others of legal affidavits from black Democrats who said they had had trouble obtaining and casting ballots. Abrams claimed that removing ineligible voters from the rolls, requiring voter identification, and matching signatures all constituted forms of "voter suppression."

By acquiescing in the settlement, Raffensperger in effect denied scrutiny of Georgia's notoriously inaccurate voter rolls, loosened the requirements for ensuring voter identification, and made it virtually impossible to reject absentee and mail-in ballots, essentially changing the absentee ballot process established by state law.

TRUMP

Previously, ballots with faulty or incorrect information were simply rejected, but the settlement allowed ballots to be "cured," or corrected after the fact. Previously, Georgia law required signatures to match the signature on file with the Georgia voter registration database. But the settlement allowed the signature to match any signature on file, including the one on the absentee ballot application. Finally, the settlement made it procedurally very difficult to reject mail-in ballots for any reason, tripling the number of people required to approve a rejection.[2]

It's one thing for left-wing activist groups to convince a Democratic secretary of state to sign such agreements, but why would a Republican secretary of state, backed by a Republican governor, do that? This is a big and unanswered question. Some Republicans in Georgia say that Kemp is a "Never Trumper" and wanted Trump to lose. Others say that Kemp and Raffensperger were intimidated by the behemoth Stacey Abrams, who continued to batter them with accusations of racism—accusations that they were desperate to avoid.

In fairness, when Raffensperger signed the consent agreement in March 2020, Covid was just arriving on the scene, and he had no idea that there would be such a sharp and dramatic rise in mail-in balloting in the November election. This massive escalation itself made careful signature matching very difficult, and with the consent decree in place it made it effectively null and avoid. This was the real reason for the startling difference in the rejection rates of mail-in ballots between 2016 and 2018 on the one hand and 2020 on the other.

Whatever their motives, it is hardly an exaggeration to say that this consent decree approved by Raffensperger, with Kemp's backing, was the enabling mechanism for the mule operation that the Democrats unleashed in Georgia in late 2020 and early 2021. Viewed retrospectively, Kemp and Raffensperger created the conditions not only for Trump's defeat in Georgia, but also for the defeat of the two

Georgia Republican candidates for the U.S. Senate, both incumbents: ✗
David Perdue and Kelly Loeffler.

As for the Trump campaign lawsuit, it was filed in Fulton County
and assigned to a progressive judge, Constance Russell, who said it
would be taken up "in due course," which as a practical matter meant
several months after Biden's inauguration. Although the Georgia
Republican Party lawyers filed an emergency appeal to the state's
supreme court, it was rejected on procedural grounds—the high court
said it was a trial court issue that needed to be adjudicated at the lower
court level—and directed back to the Fulton County courts.

The case was reassigned to Cobb County Superior Court judge
Adele Grubbs, who set a hearing date of January 8, two days after
the official certification of the Electoral College votes in the U.S.
Senate. Obviously the case would be moot by that time, so David
Shafer, chairman of the Georgia Republican Party, and his team
withdrew it. "No one wanted to touch this case with a 10-foot pole,"
Shafer said. "They were running the clock out on us."[3] And they did.

In March 2021, True the Vote filed its complaint with the secretary of state's office in Georgia, exposing widespread mule trafficking.
The complaint laid out the story in Georgia. A whistleblower came
forward and confessed to participating in and being paid for ballot
trafficking. He pointed to a network that was doing that in the state.
Catherine and Gregg provided both geotracking and video evidence.
They did not call for decertification of the Georgia election. They did
call for law enforcement to step in and bust the racket.

The Trump/Shafer lawsuit had exposed possible venues of election fraud and anomalies that warranted a closer look. But it did
not document systematic fraud. True the Vote's complaint did, using

reliable geotracking evidence and video evidence taken by the state of Georgia's official surveillance cameras.

For a month, the response from Raffensperger's office was silence. Then an investigator from the secretary of state's office reached out to True the Vote and asked for the name of the whistleblower. Catherine and Gregg informed the investigator that the whistleblower had only come forward under the assurance that his name would not be disclosed. He did not want to face the wrath of the criminal network he had served or face the risk of criminal prosecution. Catherine and Gregg told the whistleblower that he might be able to secure immunity, but he was not convinced. This information was conveyed to the secretary of state's office.

Catherine and Gregg met confidentially with representatives of Raffensperger's office and representatives of the Georgia Bureau of Investigation, including GBI director Vic Reynolds. They provided preliminary geotracking data from both the presidential election and the Georgia U.S. Senate runoffs. Later this data was augmented by further data analysis, drop box surveillance video, chain of custody documents, and other corroborating evidence.

Raffensperger's office promised to review the evidence and get back to Catherine and Gregg. For weeks, they heard nothing. Then, on October 21, 2021, an article appeared in the *Atlanta Journal-Constitution*. Written by Mark Niesse and Greg Bluestein, the article was titled "GBI Chief: Not Enough Evidence to Pursue GOP's Ballot Fraud Claim." On the face of it, this was strange. The fraud claim hadn't come from the GOP. It had come from an independent election integrity group, True the Vote.

The article quoted a letter written by GBI director Vic Reynolds to Georgia state GOP chairman David Shafer. "Based on what has been provided and what has not been provided," Reynolds said, "an investigation is not justified." Reynolds's letter continued, "What

TRUMP

has not been provided is any other kind of evidence that ties these cellphones to ballot harvesting. As it exists, the data, while curious, does not rise to the level of probable cause that a crime has been committed."

Without probable cause, Reynolds suggested, the GBI would be unable to obtain search warrants to pursue the case further. Moreover, Reynolds conveyed in his letter that even if there had been probable cause, his office had no jurisdiction to investigate or address these potential election crimes. Reynolds added: "It has been stated that there is a 'source' that can validate ballot harvesting. Despite repeated requests, that source has not been provided to either the GBI or the FBI."

The article concluded on the familiar journalistic boilerplate. "The allegation of ballot collections is only one of the wave of unverified claims that Trump lost because of illegal behavior rather than receiving fewer votes than Democrat Joe Biden. . . . State election officials have conducted multiple investigations into allegations of fraud, including audits and recounts, but none has found organized efforts to change the outcome of the presidential election."[4]

This article outraged Catherine and Gregg on a variety of fronts. First, the GBI letter had been leaked to the media. It contained information presented confidentially by True the Vote and risked compromising the identity of the people involved in Gregg's investigation. Instead of investigating the mules, the GBI had chosen to expose the names of the investigators and place them under public scrutiny.

Second, Reynolds's statements were absurd on their face. As James Bopp, True the Vote's attorney, pointed out in a response, "What is actually curious is Director Reynolds's legal analysis on probable cause, as similar information has been found to provide probably cause leading to indictments related to election crimes in other states." In other words, geotracking and video evidence are standard ways to bust election fraud, yet here was Reynolds pretending that the data and videos did not "rise to the level" of probable cause.

Contrast the feigned helplessness of Reynolds with the actions of the FBI and the Biden Department of Justice in the aftermath of the January 6 riot. Using precisely the same methods—geotracking and videos taken at the Capitol—they systematically unmasked the protesters, tracked them down, and arrested them. There was no idle rumination about the difficulty of meeting a "probable cause" standard. The presence of their phones inside the Capitol, plus the video evidence where available, was more than enough to establish probable cause. Once again, we see here how the law works one way when it benefits Democrats and another way when it benefits Republicans.

Even more idiotic was Reynolds's insistence that he had no jurisdiction over the issue. If the FBI and the GBI could not investigate systematic election fraud, who could? These are serious crimes according to Georgia's own statutes. They involve the outcome of a federal election. Quite obviously both the FBI and GBI have jurisdiction here. Yet with a straight face Reynolds insisted they did not.

Finally, Bopp's letter pointed out that "True the Vote has refrained from revealing the names of individuals who gave information, in part because of the sensitive nature of their disclosures and the physical danger to those individuals if exposed. True the Vote was concerned that despite your office's and the GBI's promises of confidentiality, that the identities of those involved would be leaked. These concerns have been confirmed by the leak of the GBI letter to the media."[5]

This might seem to be the end of the matter, but in early January 2022 investigative journalist John Solomon appeared on the Fox News Channel show *Hannity* to announce that Raffensperger's office had opened a new investigation into illegal ballot harvesting based on the evidence provided by True the Vote. This was the first

I brought Salem hosts Charlie Kirk, Eric Metaxas, and Dennis Prager into the movie by initially recording their positions on election fraud in the 2020 election and then filming their reactions as they saw the evidence assembled by True the Vote.

Among the five Salem hosts in the movie, I count Larry Elder, Dennis Prager, and Charlie Kirk as initial skeptics, while Sebastian Gorka and Eric Metaxas were inclined to the view that the 2020 election was stolen.

This captures our first meeting with Catherine Engelbrecht and Gregg Phillips, where they presented us with their evidence of geotracking and surveillance videos showing systematic election fraud.

This is a movie recreation of our fateful summit with Catherine and Gregg. We took their evidence to Salem Media to see if Salem would provide the equity investment to make the *2000 Mules* documentary.

Catherine Engelbrecht founded True the Vote because she realized that our election system is broken, with bad voter rolls creating opportunities for massive fraud.

Gregg Phillips has a deep background in election intelligence and election integrity. His team conducted the cellphone geotracking analysis using 10 trillion pings of data to reveal more than 2,000 mules visiting 10 or more mail-in drop boxes.

Elections are the lifeblood of a democracy. Without free and fair elections we are not a constitutional democracy; we are a criminal cartel masquerading as a democracy.

My wife Debbie met Catherine Engelbrecht years ago and was trained by True the Vote as a bilingual poll watcher and poll judge.

This is the set we created as a replica of Gregg Phillips's office. It was here that we filmed my in-depth interview with Catherine and Gregg that formed the spine of the documentary.

What we see here are screenshots from the videos of mules stuffing multiple ballots into mail-in drop boxes. While vote harvesting is legal in some states, typically under restricted conditions, paid ballot trafficking is illegal across the country. What you are seeing here is organized crime on behalf of the Democratic Party.

More mule videos. Notice the use of latex gloves to avoid leaving fingerprints on the fraudulent ballots, and also the mules taking photos of the drop boxes and of the ballots going in, so as to provide proof of work done in order to get paid.

This is one of True the Vote's most industrious mules, who went to multiple drop boxes across multiple counties in a single day.

This mule, whom we nicknamed Bike Guy, stuffed the ballot box and was about to take off when he remembered he forgot something. So he came back and took a picture. Why would you do that if you were merely dropping off your own ballot or the ballots of your family members?

Scott Walter, president of Capital Research Center, has tracked the huge inflow of progressive and Democratic money flowing into nonprofits. How much did Zuckerberg and the liberal donors know about the mule operation?

Hans von Spakovsky, former Federal Election commissioner, spoke about the various places left-wing nonprofits could have obtained illegal ballots, from nursing homes to public housing complexes to homeless shelters and college campuses.

This is the set at a California hotel where I filmed the Salem hosts not only reacting to the evidence of election fraud but then summing up their new perspective, shaped by what they learned from True the Vote.

The Salem lineup: Eric Metaxas, Dennis Prager, Dinesh D'Souza, Charlie Kirk, Sebastian Gorka, and Larry Elder.

This mule is from Yuma County, Arizona. She was able to be in the movie because she got busted and cooperated with authorities. Still, for her safety, she asked that her identity be concealed and her voice slightly camouflaged.

Gregg Phillips revealing how his team helped identify suspects in the murder of a young girl in Atlanta, the point being that the same type of geotracking was used to identify the 2,000-plus mules featured in the movie.

This is a casual shot of Debbie and me at our "house"—not our real house—during filming. Debbie here has achieved her goal, going back to her childhood days in Venezuela, of being a soap star. In the background is our film partner and friend Bruce Schooley.

This is the set for my daily podcast, and we included a glimpse of it in the documentary.

Trump makes his grand entrance at our May 4, 2022, red-carpet premiere at Mar-a-Lago, a sumptuous affair featuring 500 guests and, by my daughter Danielle's count, "250 VIPs."

Trump getting ready to speak before the screening of the movie. My favorite part was his running commentary to me while the movie was playing, including some references to my "very good movie voice."

I knew in writing this book and making this movie that I would incur the wrath of the Left, the Democrats, the Never Trumpers, and even some in the GOP establishment. Our destiny, however, is in our own hands; we must act to secure our elections and protect our democracy.

official confirmation that a state had formally taken action based on Catherine and Gregg's evidence.

In an article published on his website Just the News, Solomon noted that Raffensperger was responding to new information supplied by True the Vote in November 2021 that included both geolocation data and video evidence. "We do have some information," Raffensperger said, "and we are going to investigate that." He added, "If people give us, you know, credible allegations, we want to make sure that we do that. And we have that right now as an ongoing investigation."[6]

A few days later, Raffensperger stated on the CBS program *Face the Nation* that he wanted a constitutional amendment in Georgia that permitted only American citizens to vote, a tacit admission that non-citizens might have voted in 2020 and previous elections. Raffensperger also called for a nationwide ban on ballot harvesting, again giving quiet acknowledgment that such harvesting had enabled the very fraud that he had previously denied characterized the 2020 election.[7]

What has come so far of Raffensperger's investigation? Not a lot. Raffensperger seems to be moving at a tortoise's pace. By the spring of 2022 he had not yet issued subpoenas, even though he said they were forthcoming. Obviously, subpoenas are only the first step. True the Vote remains optimistic that something is going to happen—that mules will be arrested and questioned, and that the higher-ups of this Democratic fraud scheme will be indicted. I'm not so sure. If I had to bet, the Republican establishment in Georgia will let the bad guys get away with it, because that's what Republicans do. They don't rock the boat.

Why do so many Republican leaders appear to acquiesce to Democratic voter fraud? Why are their new "voter integrity" laws so modest (merely making it somewhat more difficult for the Democrats to cheat)? One big reason is that Republicans fear being called racist—the go-to accusation made by the media, woke corporations, and the Democrats whenever the Republicans put up a fight against voter fraud. But there's another reason—and it goes back more than forty years, to 1981.

In 1981, Democrats accused Republicans of voter intimidation in a gubernatorial race in New Jersey. Anxious to avoid protracted litigation, the GOP entered into a court-mandated consent decree in 1982. This severely limited the Republican Party's involvement in any poll-watching operation. Little did the Republicans realize that, without insisting on a clear end date for this settlement, they were binding themselves in a knot for four decades of elections, not only in New Jersey but across the country.

The Democrats, with their customary mercilessness, pressed the courts to keep renewing, and indeed strengthening, the terms of the settlement. It was updated in 1987, modified again in 1990, and repeatedly renewed. Only in 2018 did the settlement finally expire, allowing the GOP to resume normal poll watching.[8]

But while for decades Republicans sat, idle and helpless, on the sidelines, Democrats had been busily perfecting their election management and litigation strategies, which were given a huge opening because of the Covid pandemic. The Democrats pushed for massive changes in election rules, and Republicans were caught flat-footed. Often, they weren't even aware of what was going on.

When Gregg and Catherine met with Arizona Republican legislators to discuss voter integrity bills in 2021, they referenced a series of consent decrees signed by Arizona's secretary of state Katie Hobbs. The Republican legislators were astonished; they didn't even know about these decrees. Without informing them, the Democratic secretary of state had willingly given in to the demands of activist leftist groups to modify the state's election rules in 2020.

When Republicans saw multiple anomalies and irregularities on Election Day itself, they didn't know what to do. Despite their frenzied legal efforts, neither did the Trump campaign or the Republican National Committee. The time available to prove election fraud was very narrow. The standards for evidence were very high. Judges would obviously be reluctant to overturn election results. The Republicans had been completely outmaneuvered.

In the immediate aftermath of the election, when Catherine and True the Vote seemed largely silent, the organization was developing its own litigation strategy focused on equal protection of the laws, showing how states concentrated Zuckerberg-funded drop boxes, voter education, and get-out-the-vote campaigns in heavily Democratic precincts and neglected Republican ones. The result—or so the legal logic went—was a denial of equal protection and equal rights for Republican voters. This litigation strategy was suggested to the RNC and the Trump campaign.

Of all the lawsuits, this one probably had the best chance to succeed. But the Trump campaign went in a different direction, emphasizing procedural violations. The courts were unreceptive—indeed openly hostile—to this approach. The RNC seemed to have no legal strategy at all. It focused on raising money and doing not much of anything.

Once the election was decided and Biden took office, the RNC seemed content to issue vacuous tweets of useless protest: "There is no place in America for election fraud" and "We will not stand for Democrats changing the rules." Though they already had.

But while the RNC dozed, True the Vote launched its investigation into electoral fraud—and sure enough, there was plenty of it to be found.

CHAPTER 9

Objections and Refutations

The documentary *2000 Mules* was released in May 2022 and quickly became the most successful political documentary in a decade. In fact, it was the most successful documentary since my own *2016: Obama's America*, released in the summer of 2012. It's not easy to compare the two films since they were released in different environments. The Obama movie had a conventional theatrical release, followed a few months later by the usual DVD and home box office release.

By contrast, *2000 Mules* was my first film released in an age of censorship. This meant I couldn't put the trailer on YouTube, I couldn't buy ads on Facebook, and I didn't want the film to be on Apple iTunes or Amazon Prime—essentially, any platform that might take it down right after it was released. So we pursued an innovative marketing strategy that worked—a tribute to the content of the film and also to the intensity of interest in the subject over the past two years.

First, we had a limited theatrical release in around three hundred theaters. We rented out the theaters for two days, May 2 and May 4,

TRUMP

essentially buying all the seats at a discount. Then we sold tickets through our website, using a relatively unknown ticketing site to avoid being cancelled by the major ticketing sites. This was a big success, and most of the theaters were full.

Then we had a red-carpet premiere at Mar-a-Lago. This was a glittering event with 800 people, "250 of them VIPs," using my daughter Danielle's count. Congressman Matt Gaetz told me, "Everyone who's anyone in MAGA is here." Trump spoke, but he was expected to leave afterwards because he had already seen the film. (My family had screened it for him a couple of weeks prior since we were renting his facility for our premiere.) But after his speech, Trump requested a large bag of popcorn and sat down next to me to watch 2000 *Mules* again.

What made the experience amusing for me was Trump's commentary throughout the film. "Dinesh," he said, "That opening music. Where'd you get it?" I said, "What do you mean?" He said, "Did you buy it? Did someone compose it?" I said we had a composer. "Man," he said, "it's good." And then, a bit later, "This film is genius. It's going to be your biggest one yet."

I chuckled inwardly, because I know Trump likes to evaluate things in terms of ratings. "Low ratings CNN," that kind of thing. Finally, at the end, he said, "Dinesh, you know you have a really good voice." And then, after a pause, "It's a good thing, you know. Because if you didn't, you'd have to hire someone to do the narration for the film." I told Debbie afterward and she responded, "That Trump is too much!"

Our red-carpet premiere was followed a few days later by a virtual premiere out of a spectacular theater in Las Vegas. When I told the people at the studio that we expected a large number of sign-ups, they told me they would provide for ten thousand, which would be more than enough. To their astonishment, more than eighty thousand people bought tickets off our website. The studio had to scramble to increase its bandwidth.

But the studio regrouped, and the event was a smashing success. People from around the country participated by getting on a Zoom call to end all Zoom calls. They watched an opening program hosted by my daughter Danielle; Debbie my wife sang the national anthem; then the movie played, followed by a lively Q&A with Gregg, Catherine, Salem host Eric Metaxas, and me.

The movie was available for digital download and streaming on just two platforms, the Salem media platform called SalemNOW and also the Rumble-owned platform Locals. Locals had never done a movie before; basically, the folks there partnered with me to demonstrate that they had a viable platform for content creators to release full-length films, comedy specials, and other long-form content. The Rumble CEO Chris Pavlovski told me, "Dinesh, if we make this work with you, you will have helped to rewrite the rules of the internet." And so we did—Locals alone did nearly $5 million in streaming with 2000 *Mules*.

The early success of the movie caused independent theaters around the country to ask for us to release the movie in the normal fashion with them. So we reopened the film in four hundred theaters—mostly Cinemark and independents—and had a decent run for three weeks. Our take was an anemic sum for a theatrical run, but in this case the film had already been available for streaming and digital download, an inversion of the normal timetable for a movie release.

Through a distributor we also got our DVDs up on Walmart, where they promptly became a bestseller, and also on Amazon, where the DVD held firm at #1 of all movies and TV shows for several weeks. Altogether the film took in more than $13 million in its first six weeks, a remarkable figure for a political documentary released under such constraints.

Most important was the film's influence, which could be seen in the massive coverage in conservative media—notwithstanding the fact that Fox News Channel refused even to mention the name of the movie—and equally intense responses on social media. Remarkably, *2000 Mules* trended on Twitter for more than a week. When I noticed that *2000 Mules* wasn't trending, I saw that "Dinesh" was trending, and when I finally saw that neither Dinesh nor *2000 Mules* was trending, my wife noticed that "D'Souza" was trending. The cultural impact of the documentary can also be gauged in the success of rapper Forgiato Blow's song *2000 Mules*, which was taken down from YouTube but not before attracting hundreds of thousands of views.

The film's influence was also documented by the polling firm Rasmussen Reports in a remarkable survey conducted in June 2022. The survey found that 15 percent of voters—around 20 million people—had actually seen the film. "Among voters who have seen *2000 Mules*, 85 percent of Republicans, 68 percent of Democrats, and 77 percent of unaffiliated voters say the movie strengthened their conviction that there was systematic and widespread fraud in the 2020 election."

According to Rasmussen, "Among voters who have seen the documentary, 78 percent said they would recommend *2000 Mules* to others regardless of whether or not they share their political beliefs. That includes 84 percent of Republicans, 73 percent of Democrats and 74 percent of unaffiliated voters."[1] The stunning finding here is that the documentary not only vindicates Republicans who long suspected fraud but also persuades a clear majority of independents and Democrats that, contrary to what they have been hearing nonstop in the media, fraud on behalf of Democrats was rampant in the last presidential election.

The impact of the documentary could also be felt in Yuma County, Arizona, where Sheriff Leon Wilmot opened up a new investigation into paid ballot trafficking in the 2020 election. The sheriff said he was looking into impersonation fraud, false registrations, duplicate voting, and fraudulent use of absentee and mail-in ballots.

Following this announcement, two uniformed officers and two plainclothes investigators from the Arizona attorney general's office raided the nonprofit Comite de Bien Estar, run by a man named Tony Reyes, a Democrat and chair of the Yuma County Board of Supervisors. The search warrant permitted officers to confiscate the phone and search the home of Gloria Torres, an employee of the group who is also a member of the San Luis City Council. Torres is suspected of coordinating illegal ballot harvesting, which is a Class 5 felony.

Torres, who served for two decades on the Gadsden Elementary School Board, is a political ally of Guillermina Fuentes, a former San Luis mayor and Gadsden School Board member who faced prosecution for ballot trafficking at the time *2000 Mules* was released. Fuentes had a battery of high-profile attorneys with Democratic Party connections who were preparing her defense. Just days after the film's appearance, however, Fuentes changed her plea from "not guilty" to "guilty." Sheriff Wilmot says he is currently investigating sixteen other similar cases in Yuma County for election fraud.[2]

Agitated at the potential role of the film in driving these events, reporter Jerod MacDonald-Evoy of the *Arizona Mirror* rushed to interview the sheriff and assure his readers that "the Yuma sheriff isn't investigating election fraud because of *2000 Mules*." The article quotes the sheriff saying that his office "has been working jointly with the Yuma County Recorder's Office and the Arizona attorney general's office extensively regarding allegations of voter misconduct for over a year."[3]

But David Lara, who first recorded Guillermina Fuentes delivering multiple ballots to drop boxes, said the sheriff's office had been sitting on the investigation for eighteen months before the movie came out—and then moved on it. Lara told Chanel Rion of One America News Network that he had no doubt the film spurred both Attorney General Mark Brnovich and the Yuma sheriff to make the public announcement when they did.

Let's recall that True the Vote has been doing work in Yuma for more than a year. It was one of the first places that Gregg and Catherine developed their leads. True the Vote has provided information both to the local authorities in Yuma and to the Arizona attorney general's office. It is this information—assembled and dramatized in the film—that propelled the arrests, the raid, and the subsequent expanded investigation. Nothing the sheriff said is inconsistent with these facts.

Moreover, as I tweeted out shortly after the publication of the *Arizona Mirror* story, if the sheriff's newly announced investigation had nothing to do with *2000 Mules*, then it provided *independent confirmation* of the legitimacy of the issues shown in the documentary. Prior to the film, no one was talking about illegal ballot trafficking. Now suddenly the Arizona authorities were putting faces on the mules and showing that these are criminal violations that can and must be prosecuted.

*

Yet the very sensation caused by *2000 Mules* brought out a strong reaction from the Left. The Left's predictable initial reaction was to deny the movie's importance and to dismiss it as simply the latest conspiracy theory that did not even require a refutation. This was the approach taken by Kaleigh Rogers on the FiveThirtyEight website run by progressive pollster Nate Silver. Titled "There Is More Than One Big Lie," the article began by noting that "there's a mountain of baseless overlapping claims piled up inside the stultifying biodome of the

Big Lie: voters casting multiple ballots, dead people voting, ballot counting machines flipping votes, foreign nations hacking systems to swap totals."

The Big Lie, Rogers said, is actually a mélange of lies, an "à la carte conspiracy theory . . . where adherents pick and choose what sounds right to them and disregard what doesn't." This article appeared in February 2022 on the heels of my release of the first teaser trailer. Rogers hadn't even seen the movie. She couldn't, because it was three months away from being released.

Yet her point was that the references to geotracking evidence and video evidence in the trailer required no follow-up. They could be safely dismissed—along with all the evidence accumulated by True the Vote—and tossed into a generic garbage heap of fraud theories, essentially implying that if those theories lack evidence, then this one must also. But this doesn't follow at all; even if previous theories are inadequate, this one must be evaluated on its merits. This the article didn't do, nor did FiveThirtyEight publish any subsequent analysis that did so either.

Remarkably, the same illogic in the FiveThirtyEight article was featured in a *New York Times* article published in May 2022—after the release of the movie. Alexandra Berzon, who coauthored the article with Danny Hakim, saw the movie. I know because she attended our Mar-a-Lago premiere on May 4 where the movie was played, and I spoke to her about it. Berzon, a sulky, obese individual, bears a striking resemblance to one of the mules in the film—until she introduced herself, I wondered whether one of our mules had somehow gained entrance to the premiere.

Hakim and Berzon's article, "A Big Lie in a New Package," begins with examples intended to invite ridicule. "Votes switched by Venezuelan software. Voting machines hacked by the Chinese. Checking for telltale bamboo fibers that might prove ballots had been flown in from

Asia." None of this is from the film or has anything to do with it. Even so, for Hakim and Berzon, these examples are the prelude to "Trump showcasing his latest election conspiracy theory."[4]

I saw two separate headlines in the Daily Beast and Mediaite that essentially said the same thing. Here's the Daily Beast: "Dinesh D'Souza's Vile Big Lie Documentary Is Too Stupid Even for Fox: I watched this crap so you don't have to—and, trust me, you don't want to." Here's Mediaite: "The *Washington Post* Watched and Fact Checked Dinesh D'Souza's 2020 Election Movie So You Don't Have to." Notice here how media organizations recycle each other's fact checks. Notice also how keen the Left is that its own audience not see the movie. This could be related to the Rasmussen finding that it persuades independents and even Democrats.

Once the Left and the mainstream media realized that blithe dismissals were insufficient and a more detailed critique of the film was necessary, they unleashed their "fact-checkers" at outlets such as the Associated Press, PolitiFact, Reuters, and the *Washington Post*. Philip Bump, a national correspondent for the *Washington Post*, turned out to be the most assiduous critic of *2000 Mules*, writing no fewer than a dozen articles about it starting in early 2022 and engaging in a lengthy, combative Q&A with me that lasted an hour and ran several thousands of words on the *Post*'s website.

Criticism of the film came not only from the Left but also from the Never Trump and establishment Right. Congresswoman Liz Cheney of the January 6 Committee said during the hearings that the film had been "debunked" without offering any proof or even any sources of the so-called debunking. The Never Trump site The Dispatch featured its own fact-check proclaiming that "the film's ballot harvesting theory is full of holes," and Ben Shapiro did a detailed review on his podcast that, while not entirely unfavorable, declared the thesis of the film unconvincing on the basis of key points that I'll take up in this chapter.

***

Let's start with the common refrain in the various critiques that cellphone geotracking is not reliable enough to place mules at mail-in drop boxes. Here's Bump: "Can cellphone geolocation data differentiate between visiting a library and visiting a dropbox at that library?" Bump cites a source who claims that geotracking is accurate to "within probably 30 feet," and concludes that since "cellphones are regularly but not constantly recording your position" it follows that "a ping directly next to a dropbox outside a library might be you dropping off a ballot, or it could be you walking by on your way into a building. Or it could be you driving by on the street."[5]

Here's Ali Swenson of the Associated Press: "Experts say cellphone location data, even at its most advanced, can only reliably track a smartphone within a few meters—not close enough to know whether someone actually dropped off a ballot or just walked or drove nearby. . . . What's more, ballot drop boxes are often intentionally placed in busy areas, such as college campuses, libraries, government buildings and apartment complexes. . . . Delivery drivers, postal workers, cab drivers, poll workers and elected officials all have legitimate reasons to cross paths with numerous drop boxes or nonprofits in a given day."[6]

And here, incredibly enough, is former attorney general Bill Barr, testifying before the January 6 Committee. Barr said he was "unimpressed" with the geotracking evidence in the film, explaining himself this way: "If you take 2 million cell phones and figure out where they are physically in a big city like Atlanta or wherever, just by definition, you're going to find any hundreds of them have passed by and spend time in the vicinity of these boxes. The premise that if you go by a box, five boxes or whatever it was, you know that that's a mule is just indefensible."[7]

There are several points to be made here. First, we can verify from our own experience that cellphone geotracking is highly accurate. Here's a tweet that a guy posted on May 21, 2022: "I keep hearing people on the left say 2000 Mules is bullshit because geotracking on cell phones isn't that accurate. . . . I requested an Uber the other day at the Miami airport and my phone knew I was standing in front of door #28 at gate J."[8]

Along the same lines, a friend of mine told me he dropped his phone during a hike and couldn't find it in the tall grass. He ran a "find my phone" search on one of his other devices and voilà! It took him directly to his phone. In a mocking tone my friend said, "It didn't take me to within thirty feet of my phone. It took me straight to the phone." What makes this anecdote powerful is that any of us can verify it for ourselves by performing the same experiment.

The *New York Times* confirmed the precision of geotracking in a detailed feature in 2019 titled "One Nation, Tracked." The article used geolocation data to follow the movements of several people at the White House, the Pentagon, and even Mar-a-Lago. Sample quotation: "A single dot appeared on the screen, representing the precise location of someone in President Trump's entourage at 7:10 a.m. It lingered around the grounds of the president's Mar-a-Lago Club in Palm Beach, Fla., where the president was staying, for about an hour."

More from the same feature: "The data reviewed . . . originated from a location data company, one of dozens quietly collecting precise movements using software slipped onto mobile phone apps. . . . They can see the places you go every moment of the day, whom you meet or spend the night with, where you pray, whether you visit a methadone clinic, a psychiatrist's office or a massage parlor."[9]

Right around the time the documentary came out, there were news reports that the Center for Disease Control (CDC) had purchased cellphone data to verify if people were social distancing. Think about it: If geotracking is not accurate to within six feet, how would the CDC be able to do that? Reviewing the accuracy of geotracking in the case *Carpenter v. United States*—a case involving digital privacy that came before the Supreme Court—Chief Justice John Roberts wrote in 2018, "When the Government tracks the location of a cell phone, it achieves near perfect surveillance as if it had attached an ankle monitor to the phone's user."[10]

The conservative website Gateway Pundit interviewed tech guru David Sinclair. Sinclair is the founder of Volta Wireless, which provides software and services to stop network operators from tracking your location, identity, and internet activity. It also protects users from being geotracked by the government or tech giants. Sinclair said, "I've seen the movie. I've read the rebuttals put out by AP and others. A lot of the fact-checkers, it's clear, don't have the technical foundation for the comments that they are making."

Sinclair added, "These phones are using GPS locations. They're also using location triangulation with the towers. Triangulation is a technology that's been used for a long time to be able to determine the location of something else. You get something at one point that tracks where something is located, and you get something at another point to track where that same thing is located. And when you combine that information, you can figure out exactly where that thing is located, within a few feet."[11]

Paradoxically, the accuracy of cellphone geotracking can be confirmed from a strident critique of *2000 Mules* by a digital privacy group called the Electronic Frontier Foundation (EFF). Somewhat comically, the EFF published an article claiming, "Data Brokers and True the Vote Are the Real Villains of '2000 Mules' Movie." True the

Vote "deserves condemnation for performing wildly invasive research on thousands of people's location data without their consent or even knowledge," providing "a reminder of our need to stop the industry of shady data brokers that enabled this massive privacy invasion."[12]

I'm not entirely unsympathetic to the EFF's concern about privacy protections, but I find it interesting that the group remains largely silent while the FBI uses cellphone geotracking to bust January 6 protesters, mum while the CDC and other government agencies deploy it to monitor citizens' private behavior, and noncommittal while commercial companies use the same data for e-commerce purposes. But somehow when it's used to expose election fraud, the EFF screams foul!

The article goes on to say that cellphone GPS data is "accurate to within about 5 meters," which is about sixteen feet—about twice the accuracy that Bump claimed in his *Washington Post* article. So the EFF's complaint undercuts the left-wing fact-checkers. The EFF is not saying that cellphone geotracking is inaccurate. On the contrary, the EFF is saying that because it's so accurate, groups like True the Vote should not be able to use it to monitor other people's behavior.

Fine, but all True the Vote did here was use the technology already used in so many other areas and apply it to ballot trafficking. Moreover, Gregg Phillips says that cellphone geotracking is far more accurate than even the EFF says. Gregg testified that it can be accurate to within eighteen inches under favorable conditions. But the general validity of True the Vote's research holds, whether the correct answer is eighteen inches, sixteen feet, or thirty feet. Even the most skeptical view of the precision of geolocation data is not enough to discredit what True the Vote found about the mules.

Why? Because True the Vote used the very high bar of requiring that mules go to ten or more drop boxes and five or more left-wing nonprofits. What reason is there to be within thirty feet of ten or more drop boxes and multiple vote stash-houses? Let's remember that mail-in drop boxes exist for the sole purpose of putting in ballots. These are not U.S. Post Office mailboxes where you might go multiple times to drop off bills and mail letters. There is only one reason to go to a mail-in drop box, and that is to insert (or, if you are an election worker, remove) ballots.

As I discussed this issue on social media, a leftist erupted at me, saying that he could use my cellphone data to show that I was in the vicinity of several gay bathhouses. How would you like it, he asked, if I accused you of patronizing gay bathhouses using the proof that your cellphone had been detected within a measurable distance from those venues? I replied that if my cellphone could be located within, say, thirty feet of ten or more gay bathhouses within a two-week period, it would be reasonable to conclude I was a regular customer.

True the Vote even compared the pattern of life of these mules during the election period—October 1, 2020, through Election Day—with their pattern of life before and after this period, to see if for some bizarre unexplained reason they habitually visited these exact same locations. Turns out, they didn't. In other words, these were traffickers going on routes to mail-in drop boxes, not ordinary citizens taking nocturnal walks or returning books to public libraries.

Anyone who is familiar with cellphone geotracking knows that there is a difference between going by or past an object and going directly to that object. The difference can be easily spotted by plotting the cellphone movements of an individual in the form of a moving dot on a graph. It is easy to tell whether the dot moves past a drop box—either slowly, if the person is walking, or rapidly, if he or she is driving—or whether it goes to the drop box, pauses there, then retreats back to where it came from—typically back to a car—and then on to the next drop box. There is even an obvious difference (to use Philip Bump's chosen example) between visiting a library or visiting a drop box located outside that library.

This is the distinction that Bill Barr seems to be unaware of. He mistakenly thinks that random people walking or driving by drop boxes will somehow be erroneously counted as mules. Nonsense! Using Barr's logic—or perhaps I should say illogic—since there are hundreds of thousands of people in Washington, D.C., going around and past and by the Capitol, the FBI has no way to individually identify January 6 protesters and say that this particular one was just outside the door of the Capitol, or this other one was several feet inside the door. But the Biden administration Department of Justice's charging documents certainly make such claims, and one would think as the country's chief law enforcement officer Bill Barr would be familiar with the capabilities of technology routinely used to help solve crimes and prosecute criminal cases.

Barr isn't just ignorant of geotracking; he also seems ignorant of what the movie actually showed. Barr twice said he was looking for "photographs" showing the same mule at multiple locations, but the documentary in fact doesn't show any photographs. Rather, it shows surveillance videos taken by the states themselves. When I heard Barr's comments, I thought to myself, "Has this guy even seen the film? How irresponsible of him to testify about a film he hasn't watched, at least not very attentively."

I had a similar feeling when I read Ali Swenson's AP article. Considering the types of videos shown in the movie, what sense can we make of Swenson's writing that the mules could be cabdrivers, delivery drivers, postal workers, poll workers, or elected officials? Cabdrivers might drive by drop boxes, but why would they have to go to them? The same applies to delivery drivers. Elected officials have no reason to visit multiple drop boxes.

Poll workers, of course, do—but only to remove ballots. The mules we see in the videos aren't taking out ballots or filling out custody documents; rather, they can be seen stuffing multiple ballots into the boxes. So these are preposterous examples, and are quite obviously absurd to anyone who has actually seen the movie.

·•·

Tom Dreisbach of NPR decided to attack *2000 Mules* another way, a sort of sideways attack. His article was titled "A Pro-Trump Film Suggests Its Data Are So Accurate, It Solved a Murder. That's False."[13] Notice that even in the headline Dreisbach seeks to impugn the documentary by calling it a "pro-Trump" film. Trump appears in the film for around sixty seconds out of ninety minutes. The film is about the integrity of our elections, not about Trump, although of course Trump was the candidate cheated out of the presidency in 2020.

Let's dive into Dreisbach's fact-check, because it is such a classic of the genre. Notice the premise: *2000 Mules* claims to have solved a murder. In the film, Gregg Phillips shows a circle on a map containing the "only legitimate shooters" and then says he "turned the bulk of this information over to the Federal Bureau of Investigation." I say, "Now, I read they've arrested two suspects." Phillips responds, "They have."

Now, where in this exchange do either Gregg or I claim to have solved a murder? How does identifying the cellphone IDs of potential shooters by itself identify the killer? Obviously, it has led to possible suspects. Obviously, this information is helpful to law enforcement. Obviously, law enforcement must determine which of these cellphone IDs point to the actual perpetrator or perpetrators. Thus by setting up a straw man—these guys claim to have solved a murder—Dreisbach can then contend: Well, actually, they didn't.

Dreisbach's smoking gun—at least in his mind—is his claim that True the Vote conveyed its geotracking information to the FBI in October 2021, while "authorities in Georgia arrested and secured indictments against two suspects in the murder of Secoriea Turner in August 2021." So? In what way is this information inconsistent with anything in the film?

Is Dreisbach implying that the geotracking information is useless because it was provided after the arrests? Prosecutors and investigators routinely continue their investigation even after arresting suspects. New information uncovered after an arrest is often used at trial to help establish the guilt of the accused. The only point True the Vote and I were making here is that the very same geotracking that can help identify murder suspects was used to identify mules engaged in ballot trafficking.

Dreisbach presses on. "NPR contacted the GBI," he writes—this is the Georgia Bureau of Investigation—to fact-check the claim that Gregg and Catherine did in fact provide information to them. Dreisbach quotes Nelly Miles, the GBI director of the Office of Public and Governmental Affairs. "The GBI did not receive information from True the Vote that connected to the Secoriea Turner investigation." Dreisbach lays it on by adding, "An attorney for Secoriea Turner's family told NPR they had never heard of Engelbrecht's and Phillips' analysis either."

Yet in the film Gregg Phillips unmistakably says he provided the geotracking information to the FBI, not the GBI. These are entirely different organizations, with separate offices and separate personnel, carrying out separate investigations and inquiries. The only way to refute Gregg would be to ask the FBI. Dreisbach did, and the FBI said it does not comment on its sources.

So Dreisbach decided to get his GBI denial, in the full confidence that his audience would either miss the distinction or willingly go

ACLED
ARMED CONFLICT LOCATION + EVENT DATA PROJECT

along with his bogus rebuttal. Moreover, what does Secoriea Turner's family have to do with any of this? Do agencies like the FBI and GBI routinely share their sources of technical information with the aggrieved family in murder cases? Of course not. So a family's statement to the effect of "We don't know anything about this" is meaningless.

Dreisbach is not done. He now takes up Gregg's contention in the film that there is a substantial overlap between the population of ballot-trafficking mules and that of violent rioters connected with groups such as Antifa and BLM. Since Gregg referred in the film to a group called ACLED, Dreisbach rushes to get what he can from the group's representatives.

"This is not the type of analysis you can use ACLED data for, and it's highly unlikely that these conclusions have any basis in fact," says Sam Jones, senior communications manager at ACLED. Roudabeh Kishi, director of research, adds, "This is not what we do—we do not track device IDs."

Well, let's see. Dreisbach emailed Catherine about what the ACLED representatives told him, and Catherine responded showing him ACLED documents noting that "the ACLED project codes report information on the type, agents, location, date and other characteristics of political violence events. . . . ACLED focuses on tracking a range of violent and non-violent actions by political agents, including governments, rebels, militias, identity groups, political parties, external actors, rioters, protesters and civilians."

In sum, ACLED provides highly precise and detailed information on riots and rioters. Catherine wrote, "Gregg's team researched the politically relevant violent events in our areas of study, isolated project code data using ACLED, aggregated IMEIs that were within the location at the time identified by ACLED, reconfirmed coordinates with other data sources, then compared and matched with IMEIs identified

INTERNATIONAL MOBILE EQUIPMENT
IDENTITY

in our broader ballot trafficking study."[14] In other words, ACLED provided everything except the cellphone IDs, and True the Vote used its own cellphone database—the database with the 10 trillion pings—to identify those and make the relevant comparison.

Now we turn to the video evidence, which poses a serious problem for those on the Left because they cannot deny that the video is the official surveillance video of the states themselves, nor is it easy to contest things that an audience can see for itself. Even so, the fact-checkers refuse to be deterred, raising objections both to my interpretation of mules' taking photos of the ballots going into the boxes as well as to Gregg's reading of the significance of mules' wearing gloves at some point during the Georgia runoffs.

Let's start with the photos. Here's an excerpt of my exchange with Philip Bump that appeared in the *Washington Post*.

> **Bump:** Do you have evidence . . . that these people needed to take a picture in order to get paid?
>
> **D'Souza:** Yes. . . . The way the whole investigation got started is that True the Vote had a hotline and they were approached by a whistleblower in Atlanta who said he was dropping off ballots, he was getting paid $10 a ballot and he described that he was not alone, but he was part of a larger operation. So you have direct testimony to the effect that this is a paid operation.
>
> **Bump:** Except that it's not. In the movie, you don't make this case. . . . You don't present this whistleblower.
>
> **D'Souza:** True the Vote submitted reports . . . to Georgia long before the movie. So the movie is a part of all

this, but the movie is also a movie. There are things that you can't do in a movie that are nevertheless being done on the ground that are part of the research process.

Bump: I want to go back to this issue of taking pictures of the ballot. . . . Now you recognize that a lot of people took photos of themselves voting in the 2020 election.

D'Souza: If they were taking photos of themselves, you could then argue they're taking a selfie to demonstrate that they voted. But I think it's quite obvious from the footage itself that they're taking photos of the ballots going in, and that's a whole different matter.[15]

Bump's line of contention is matched here by Reuters, whose fact-checker insisted that "clips show men in separate locations taking photos of themselves posting their ballot, which the documentary makers allege was to provide evidence of the job done so the 'mules' can get paid."[16]

This is simply dishonest. There is not a single video in the film of a mule taking a picture of himself or herself. In every case, the mules are taking pictures of the drop box or of the ballots going into the drop box. It is this telling detail—combined, of course, with the report of the whistleblower—that makes it obvious the mules are doing this to prove their presence at the drop box and that they got the job done so that they can get paid. In the case of the so-called bike guy, he forgot to take the picture, so he came back and then took a photo, again not of himself but of the drop box.

Reuters, along with several other fact-checkers, also takes up the issue of several mules who are shown during the Georgia runoffs wearing gloves. Ali Swenson, the AP fact-checker, had inanely suggested that "voting in Georgia's January 5, 2021, Senate runoff election occurred during some of the coldest weeks of the year in the state," and so quite likely the gloves could be explained by the "cold weather."[17] This could hardly fly since every mule shown is wearing *latex* gloves, not woolen or leather gloves. Is it common practice to wear blue latex gloves to keep our hands warm in the winter? I can't believe Swenson had actually seen the movie when she wrote this.

Reuters, however, knows it needs a more sophisticated explanation, and so we get this. "The documentary makers did not appear to consider the possibility that the woman was wearing gloves . . . as a personal protective measure against Covid-19."[18] Well, yes, we did consider this possibility. But we dismissed it on two grounds. First, every mule wearing gloves immediately discards the gloves once the ballots go into the box, typically tossing the gloves into a nearby trash can. But if ballot drop boxes can transmit Covid, so, presumably, can many other things that the mules might touch. So why wouldn't Covid-alert people keep their gloves on?

Second—and more significant—mules who appear on video between October 1 and Election Day aren't wearing gloves. Even in the Georgia runoffs, mules aren't wearing gloves before mid-December 2020. They only appear with latex gloves after that. This is an anomaly that requires explanation. Gregg's explanation is that the gloves appear the very day after an Arizona indictment in which the FBI busted some Democratic ballot traffickers in part because of their fingerprints on multiple ballots. So, quite obviously, the word went out among the mules: start wearing gloves!

This is not only the best but the only explanation that makes sense of the facts before us. Yet Khaya Himmelman of The Dispatch idiotically echoes the Covid-19 gloves explanation, adding lamely, "As he does throughout the film, D'Souza chooses the most nefarious explanation of an event as the only explanation without bothering to explain why other plausible explanations must be ruled out."[19]

Now we turn to perhaps the most serious allegation launched against the film, one stressed by Ben Shapiro and echoed by others. Where is the video footage of the same mule at multiple drop boxes? "None of the surveillance videos showed the same person more than once," Reuters wrote. My answer in this case is not to dispute the point raised, but to show why it is an unreasonable demand to make of the movie.

The reason is the shocking paucity of video surveillance footage taken by the states—in particular the five states under investigation here. The entire state of Wisconsin took no surveillance footage. It was required to take it, said it was going to, but didn't. True the Vote has to date been unable to obtain any footage out of Pennsylvania. Some footage may exist, but none has been obtained yet.

In Michigan, there is very limited footage. In Arizona, the same. In Maricopa County there were surveillance cameras, but most of them were turned off. No explanation has been provided for who did this or why. Even in Georgia, where True the Vote obtained most of its video, many counties did no surveillance at all. Others said they didn't have it or couldn't provide it. Still others provided it but only for a very limited period, a tiny fraction of early voting and Election Day in the presidential election and the runoffs.

Even when video footage was provided, much of it was of very poor quality. Some of the cameras weren't even pointed at the drop boxes. Others captured such grainy footage that it is impossible to recognize the faces of the mules. I actually do have footage of the same mule at more than one drop box. I chose not to use it in the movie because you can't clearly tell it's the same guy. Yes, he has the same height and build, but audiences need to see that the two guys have the same face. I know it's the same guy, but not because of his appearance; rather, I know because it's the same cellphone ID at both locations.

On social media I did release an image of the same mule on two separate occasions in two different outfits at the same drop box. Why the same drop box? Because that is one of the relatively few drop boxes that had video surveillance. So this is the point. Had the states followed the rules and done their jobs, it would be easy to find mules not just at two or three but at ten or more locations. In fact, we would be able to tell by cellphone geotracking when mules arrived at each destination and then capture them on video at those locations.

It is the failure of the states to install the cameras that explains my inability to provide what Ben Shapiro and the other critics want. But let me show by way of an analogy why their demand is excessive, and why what I have shown adequately makes the case. Consider a serial killer who has gone in a single night to five homes and killed five different people. Now the question before us is, what evidence would we reasonably demand to be satisfied that he did this?

Let's say the serial killer left his DNA at each of the five homes. Now obviously in this analogy I am using human DNA. In our case, we are talking about digital DNA, namely the unique and distinctive ID of a cellphone. Both, however, are equally reliable in placing the alleged perpetrator at the scenes of the crimes. Now let's assume that only one of the five homes had video surveillance. This matches my contention that only one of every ten or even twenty drop boxes had properly installed surveillance cameras.

So we review the serial killer's cellphone, and we can tell from the geotracking that he arrived at home number 5 at 2:15 a.m. We look on the surveillance camera and, sure enough, we can see the guy in that home at the expected time. Now along comes Ben Shapiro—serving, let's say, on the jury—who asks, "Where is the video of the guy at the other homes?" The obvious answer is, "We can't show you that video because it doesn't exist. It doesn't exist because those homes didn't have proper video surveillance."

Yet if we can establish for sure that the man was in fact at those locations—and his DNA is sufficient to do that—and moreover if we can confirm that in the one case where there is video, it corroborates the geotracking or digital DNA, haven't we fully proven our case? I think yes. I'm not sure about what courts of law would require in this instance, but in terms of convincing a reasonable observer that the guy was there at those venues, I feel confident in saying that's been adequately demonstrated, even in the absence of video at all the locations.

Finally, let's take up the claim that the paid ballot trafficking depicted in the film and described in this book is perfectly legal. This claim is made in various forms. Here is Khaya Himmelman in the Never Trump publication The Dispatch: "Ballot harvesting occurs when a third party collects and returns absentee or mail-in ballots on behalf of voters. Many states allow third parties to deliver ballots." The Dispatch quotes David Becker, executive director of the Center for Election Innovation and Research, as saying, "That's entirely legal."[20]

A similar point is made by Philip Bump of the *Washington Post*, who insists that the central theme of the documentary "wasn't that voters committed fraud. It is instead that Republicans don't like how those votes got to be counted." Bump, who is a little smarter than Himmelman, knows that it's not enough to say that "many states" permit ballot harvesting; we need to examine the rules of the five states in question.

Bump concedes that "collecting ballots on behalf of other people is limited under Georgia law, and anyone who might have done so possibly faces criminal prosecution." Even so, Bump writes, "There's no evidence now that such an effort in any way affected the outcome in Georgia beyond getting more legal ballots returned." Bump hammers in his point further by contending that "a voter casting a legal vote that is then submitted illegally . . . is still a legal vote." There's no election-stealing going on, Bump concludes, "unless you believe that making it easier for Trump opponents to vote is stealing an election."[21]

There is so much concealment and prevarication here that it requires some unpacking. First, the magnitude of ballot trafficking in Georgia, as in other states, is more than enough to have altered the election result. This is decisively shown in an earlier chapter of this book, and it was also shown in the movie.

Second, Bump implies that perhaps the Georgia mules seen on video depositing multiple ballots into drop boxes are merely delivering the votes of their immediate family members. Yet even if these mules have large families, why wouldn't they drop the votes in a single drop box? Why go to ten or more? Why do it in the middle of the night? Why use gloves? Why take photos of the ballots going in the box? Bump has no answers, and neither do any of the other fact-checkers that have made this same point.

Third, Bump presumes that the trafficked votes are all legitimate ballots and that the nonprofit organizations are merely delivering them as a sort of public service, "making it easier for Trump opponents to vote" in Bump's formulation. But why would ordinary citizens casting honest ballots turn them over to left-wing activist organizations? How would those organizations get hold of hundreds of thousands of ballots?

If indeed they are helping Trump opponents to cast their votes, as Bump says, they are violating IRS rules which strictly forbid nonprofits to engage in partisan election activity. Moreover, it is illegal in every state to pay mules or anyone to cast or deliver a vote. Even states with the most permissive vote-harvesting rules, such as California, don't allow that.

And this is the key point: Ballots that are trafficked in this way are illegal ballots, no matter how they are obtained. As I've shown, these ballots are most likely acquired from public-housing residents who simply handed over their ballots, campuses where students have graduated and moved away, homeless shelters where it's easy to obtain ballots for people who'll never know they voted, incapacitated residents of nursing homes who are too ill to know what's going on, or ineligible voters who died or moved out of state but whose names remain on the voter rolls.

These are all ballots that should not be counted, not only because they are for the most part fraudulent votes, but because even when they are not, the process of acquiring and delivering them has been contaminated. One of the key terms in election integrity is "chain of custody." This means ensuring a safe track for ballots from the voter's own hands all the way through the final counting process. Chain of custody is a vital part of ensuring the legitimacy of votes cast in person, and it's just as important—in some respects more so—when absentee or mail-in ballots are involved.

Here, quite obviously, the chain of custody has been broken. Ballots have found their way into the possession of activist groups with a stake in the outcome of the election. How can we be sure those ballots have not been altered or filled in by the activists themselves? How do we know they represent the authentic choice of eligible voters? We do not and cannot. No one can have confidence in the legitimacy of those ballots.

Moreover, when payment is involved, either to the voter or to a third party, the ballot is automatically rendered invalid, because now there is an issue of bribery. Thus the mule operation by itself is decisive. No state—I've made this point before, but I repeat it here—no matter how permissive its laws on vote harvesting, permits either voters or mules to be paid to cast and deliver votes. Consequently, counting those ballots constitutes election fraud and, when the number of those ballots is enough to make the difference, renders the outcome of the election itself untrustworthy and unreliable.

This is not my view; this is the view of every court and adjudicating authority that has considered the subject. In 2018, as we've seen, the result of a congressional election in North Carolina was overturned because of ballot trafficking—the same type of trafficking that is the subject of 2000 *Mules*. Even when courts have refused to overturn elections, their reason has been that there are not enough illegal ballots to change the outcome. No court has ever held that ballots illegally cast through paid operatives are nevertheless valid votes that should be counted.

CHAPTER 10

How to Fix
Election Fraud

W hat the critics and the "fact-checkers" want to cover up is nothing less than the biggest election scandal in American history. Never before has a U.S. presidential election been so deeply corrupted by coordinated fraud across multiple key states. Never before have so many people been "in" on the heist: litigating to create the conditions for it, financing it, organizing it, and then carrying it out. The mules, let us remember, are only the tail end of the operation.

The consequence—let us face it squarely—is that the wrong man is in the White House. Joe Biden is president because the Democrats stole the election from Trump, and they did it through organized cheating in the main urban areas of at least five key states. They might have cheated elsewhere too, and in other ways, but the cheating we have shown through the operation of mules in select counties in five swing states was alone sufficient to have put Biden over the top and to have given the Democrats Georgia's two U.S. Senate seats, making the Democrats majority in the Senate, which is dependent on the tie-breaking vote of Vice President Kamala Harris, also the direct product of election fraud. The only question now is, what can be done about all this?

What makes the whole scheme maddening is that the Democrats who organized it knew that it would be hard to discover the evidence of their culpability, and even if it was found, they calculated that it would be virtually impossible to do anything afterward to overturn the result, and very unlikely that they would be prosecuted for their actions. In a sense, they counted on Republican ineptitude, Republican pusillanimity, and Republican reluctance to cause a scene. They are still counting on it. "So now you know. Well, what are you going to do about it?" This is a dare that Republicans dare not turn away from. They must do something about it. If they do not, they are sealing their own electoral doom and selling out the country they profess to love.

The truth is important not merely so that we know it, not merely so that it provides vindication for those who long suspected something like this, but also because it provides a spur to action. Already many states have passed, or are in the process of considering, voter integrity laws that require voter ID, or tighten the signature verification requirements, or get rid of mail-in drop boxes, or outlaw private money from invading election offices and paying for the whole infrastructure around mail-in ballots and drop boxes.

For the Democrats, voter integrity laws are pointless because there is no need to tighten up the standards if the 2020 election was the most secure election of all time, as they constantly, stridently insist. Since it was so secure, the system is working beautifully; and since there is no problem, there is no need for a solution. Moreover, from this perspective, those pushing for a solution must have an ulterior motive, and that motive quite obviously is voter suppression. Republicans are against democracy because they are trying to block minorities and the poor from exercising their legitimate right to vote.

This, then, is the logical chain that leads to the absurd chant that voter integrity laws are Jim Crow 2.0. Indeed, the Democrats have been pushing to fight Jim Crow 2.0 by passing their own slate of laws aimed, they say, at saving democracy. "Saving democracy" is now the mantra, echoed in the media as a robotic chant. We are now in the surreal position of watching the very people who subverted democracy in the 2020 election pose as its guardians and saviors. Somehow the arsonist has turned up wearing the uniform of the firefighter.

The Biden Democrats are aggressively pushing to federalize the election process. They want to expand mail-in voting. They want to prevent states from imposing voter ID laws. They want to further restrict signature matching and other measures that supposedly limit the democratic process. They want to authorize and legitimate vote harvesting. Essentially, they want to legalize their fraud. Books like this would become unnecessary because what the crooks and the crooked party are doing would then be perfectly legal.

Yet they insist they are the apostles of democracy, and they would be if their chain of reasoning were sound. But it is not sound. In fact, their whole chain of reasoning is absurd because the premise is absurd. This was not the most secure election ever; in fact, it was the most corrupt election in modern times, if not in U.S. history. If the evidence presented in this book and the accompanying movie is sound, then voter integrity laws are not only reasonable, they are an imperative to save democracy. Democracy hangs in the balance not because of Republican voter suppression but because of systematic cheating on the part of the Democrats.

Election integrity laws, however, are not enough. Indeed, laws by themselves are not enough. More is needed to stop coordinated election fraud from happening again. What's needed is action on the part of independents and honest Democrats. Honest Democrats must reassess their allegiance to a party that carries the democratic name but subverts democratic elections. Independents must resolve to punish that party for its actions at the ballot box.

But the main responsibility lies with Republicans: Republican state legislatures, Republican secretaries of state and attorneys general, the Republican National Committee, Republican activists, and even the ordinary Republican voter. This is, in a sense, frightening, because it means that our fate is in our hands—we are responsible, we have to *do* something—but it is also empowering, because we are in a position to save ourselves and our country. But how? Yes, we must do more, but what precisely can we do?

◆

Harmeet Dhillon is a prominent attorney in San Francisco, former chair of the San Francisco Republican Party, and current chairwoman of the Republican National Lawyers Association. She is an expert in election law. I've known Harmeet since she was an undergraduate at Dartmouth. She volunteered as a writer for the *Dartmouth Review*, a renegade conservative campus newspaper.

Although I had graduated by then and was working in Washington, D.C., I still served on the board of the newspaper. Hence I crossed paths with Harmeet in her salad days, and—funny thing—Harmeet is in many respects exactly the same now as she was then. I interviewed her for the movie *2000 Mules*, and although for complex reasons I didn't use the interview in the movie, I'm featuring it here.

Dinesh: Harmeet, it seems like there's a psychological difference between Republicans and Democrats when it comes to elections. Republicans focus on the campaign. Democrats focus more on the election process itself.

Harmeet: Yeah, I think that's absolutely right. And we've seen the downfall of that approach in the 2020 election.

Dinesh: Democrats, it seems, <u>took advantage of Covid</u> to do things that they have long wanted to do.

Harmeet: Democrats seized on Covid and on restrictions that both Republican and Democrat lawmakers and governors had made in the states to effectively do by fiat what they had not been able to do either through federal legislation or—through the proper way to do this—by changing the law through the normal legislative process in the states.

Dinesh: So how did they do that?

Harmeet: In states with strong emergency powers like California, the legislature wasn't involved at all. The governor simply met with the secretary of state and, by fiat, announced new rules for our elections and our voting. He basically waived all the normal rules and put into place things that weren't there before.

Dinesh: In some cases it also seems the Democratic activists would find a Democratic secretary of state and enter into a consent decree in which, although in theory they were adversaries in a legal process, in fact they were kind of working together.

Harmeet: Well, that's a way the Democrats can do it. In some cases they didn't necessarily have to go that way, because they had judges willing to do it. They had governors, including red state governors, willing to enter into these arrangements. It was Republicans who entered into a consent decree in Georgia that significantly loosened Georgia's protections on election integrity and led to some of the chaos, the utter chaos you saw in the 2020 election in Georgia.

Dinesh: What do you think would cause Republicans to do that?

Harmeet: <u>No one wants to be called a racist</u>, okay? And so this is the trope that white politicians like Chuck Schumer and white lawyers like Marc Elias have hijacked the civil rights movement to claim that, even though for generations in the United States it's been fair and free for people of color, immigrants, minorities, you name it, women, poor people to vote in our country, they claim that's not the case. They claim Republicans are trying to send us back to the Jim Crow era. They use this racially inflammatory rhetoric and, not wanting to be called names like that, Republicans wave the white flag.

Dinesh: I mean, the irony is those Jim Crow voter suppression tactics were used by the Democratic Party.

Harmeet: Absolutely right. I grew up in rural North Carolina. It was the Democrats that were imposing segregation and poll taxes and other methods of making it difficult for former slaves—and then just minorities and poor people—to vote. Literacy tests and so forth. That wasn't introduced by Republicans. So yes, they have very quickly flipped the script, and now Republicans are on the defensive—for no reason. Election integrity works for everybody.

Dinesh: For Republicans who want to fix the process going forward, let's talk about some of the things they can do.

Harmeet: One thing to know is that a lot of Americans, they focus on the federal races or even just president. Nobody pays much attention to who's your assemblyman or your state senator or your secretary of state. But actually that's where the majority of American election laws are made.

I think it's fair to say that the laws are going to be different in California than they are in Texas. That's okay, under our constitutional scheme. But that's just the starting point. You can pass the best laws in the country. Like Georgia, Arizona, Montana have all passed election integrity laws. But if you don't have lawyers who are willing to step in and defend the state—be it the attorney general or private lawyers who step in and defend these statutes—then you lose in front of judges. Unelected federal or state judges can effectively override the election laws if they are not competently defended.

But there are other things that can be done as well. Citizens can volunteer at various levels, either through the party apparatus or through nonprofit groups. One of the biggest shortcomings of the 2020 elections was that many swing state jurisdictions—particularly big cities in Pennsylvania, Wisconsin, Michigan, Arizona, Nevada—they blocked observers from being able to observe the counting. And really, he who counts the votes decides the outcome of the election. So we should not let that pass in upcoming elections. It's critical that citizen observers be allowed to observe in a meaningful way and then be able to question and challenge irregularities—the kind of irregularities that were rife in the 2020 election.

Dinesh: It seems that the Democrats are pushing to federalize the whole process, taking it out of the hands of ordinary citizens.

Harmeet: Our elections in the U.S. have a critical role for citizens. Back in rural North Carolina, my mom, a fairly new citizen, was an observer as a Republican in Johnston County of what was happening there at the polls. That's our right as citizens. With schemes like ballot harvesting and so-called vote centers, the Democrats are effectively eliminating precincts.

Precincts are where the local volunteers or the local poll workers happen to know who you are. Even without voter ID, they know who you are, and they would know if something was fishy. When all of the checking happens at the county or state level, not at the local precinct level, all of a sudden all those local checks and balances are gone. We must insist on a return to that local control of elections.

Dinesh: Harmeet, when was the 2020 election lost?

Harmeet: In many states, the 2020 election was lost well before Election Day, in the months before. When the Mark Zuckerberg money came in and decided who was going to be staffing those county and precinct election offices. When the rules were loosened to allow different ways of returning the ballots—the ballot drop boxes and the ballot harvesting. When privately decisions were made but not communicated to the public about keeping observers so far away—football fields away from where the counting was occurring—that it was effectively meaningless. That's when it became impossible for Republicans to win in those battleground states.

Dinesh: What you're saying is that the heist of the bank was made possible when they called off the security guards and turned off the surveillance cameras and told the tellers, stop matching the signatures on the checks.

Harmeet: Absolutely. It happened with Republicans not focusing on the nuts-and-bolts aspects of who is going to count the votes. Not just getting the votes, but who is going to count them and how are we going to be sure that the count is accurate. So what Republicans need to do going forward is devote as much or more attention to the process of the elections, and not just in the month of the election, but in the months and years between elections, to make sure we don't have this situation again.

We need to ban outside money from coming in and determining the outcome of our elections. Ensure that citizens are allowed to make sure the vote counting is accurate and there is an audit trail for that. Make sure there's a match between the person who registered to vote and happens to be verified as a citizen entitled to vote in that jurisdiction and who actually voted that ballot. Making sure there's a meaningful remedy for people who violate our election laws by voting twice, forging signatures, falsely registering to vote at commercial or multiple jurisdictions, voting in more than one state.

Dinesh: The ordinary guy—and I'm no different—just thinks of voting as walking into a booth, pulling the curtain, filling out the ballot, and that's it. What you're saying is that the process, which we've taken for granted, is now precarious and needs our attention and our activism to protect it.

Harmeet: Absolutely. At every level people can get involved in the process. At a very minimum, you can get involved as an observer of the ballot counting. But beyond that I encourage Republicans, and anybody who cares about the outcome of our elections, to sign up to be an actual poll worker. Poll workers are also hired throughout the country. They are temporary workers. And they go in and actually do the job. They have to be nonpartisan in that effort, but at least they'll get their hands wet and know exactly what's going on. They can blow the whistle if they see anything untoward happening. So it's critical we have that sunshine.

Like Harmeet, Catherine Engelbrecht and Gregg Phillips are also all about fixing the process. Catherine's emphasis, different from Harmeet's, is on cleaning up the voter rolls and keeping an eye on what happens at those mail-in drop boxes. Here is an excerpt of my conversation with her about improving election integrity.

Dinesh: What can citizens do to clean up the voter rolls?

Catherine: In most states there are provisions called citizen challenges or elector challenges. Those allow a citizen from a county or municipality to challenge an ineligible record, which essentially means bringing it to the attention of their county. Maybe the person has moved, maybe the person is deceased, maybe there's a duplicate entry. There's a variety of reasons. But basically it's bringing it to the attention of the county. This is important because many counties, surprisingly, can't clean up their voter rolls because they are under consent decrees or they are facing lawsuits. There are a host of reasons things don't operate like they should. And the antidote is citizen involvement.

Dinesh: But how does a citizen know about any of this? Are you saying that if my neighbor moves to South Dakota, I can notify the county and say, "Hey, Mr. Smith is no longer living next door. He's now in South Dakota. I want you to check and make sure he's no longer on your rolls." Can you do that?

Catherine: It's quite literally that simple. Now True the Vote has a program and we do this at scale. We help to organize the data and we do it in a methodical way. But yes, citizens should do our part to make sure that our local elections have accurate data, are fully staffed, and that we participate in as many places and times and ways that we can. That changes things. Observation and participation change things.

Dinesh: Now I have my podcast, so what if I were to tell my podcast audience, "Hey guys. In the week or two weeks leading up to the election, assuming there's early voting, take your trusty cellphone and mosey down to the local drop box. Park your car and get a couple of cheeseburgers and large Cokes, and just turn your cellphone on and record everything that happens at that drop box, for as long as you don't mind hanging out there. And then when you leave, make sure someone else comes and takes your place." Can I do that?

Catherine: Yes, but I would suggest that a more efficient path is to demand of our elected leaders to equip those drop boxes with surveillance cameras and then livestream them. Just keep it transparent. And people can watch the boxes for themselves. This way we remove that veil of mystery around what's really happening.

⋅⋙⋅

This is all fine as far as it goes, but does it go far enough? Notwithstanding all our talk about reform—about preventing the fraud from happening again—there's a bigger issue here, the elephant in the living room, and I don't want to end without addressing it. What about the fraud that happened already? I raised the question at the very beginning: If you steal a country, don't you have to give it back? I now take up that question in its full significance.

Recently Catherine, Gregg, and I did a presentation before a group of members of the Republican National Committee. This was in Memphis in late April 2022. Gregg and Catherine gave the RNC members present a preview of their evidence, and the reaction was tumultuous. Many erupted with something to the effect of, "I knew it!" One or two said they had come to the event skeptical but were now forced to reexamine their previous confidence in the security of the election.

Then the discussion turned to the question that Lyndon Johnson liked to ask at the end of meetings, "And therefore what?" What followed was a lively and productive discussion of various steps that could be taken by the RNC and others. What caught my attention, however, was the first line of Catherine's response. She began by saying, "We are not trying to overturn the results of the 2020 election."

Here I felt a primal impulse, probably similar to the one felt by those January 6, 2021, protesters who went to D.C., to interrupt and yell, "Well, why not? Why should we confirm a fraudulent election? Why not overturn the election result if it was illegitimate?" I recognized that my impulse was an immediate, emotional, and somewhat primitive one. It might not, perhaps, reflect my considered judgment. Yet as I thought about it, I realized that it wasn't wrong to feel this way. Why should someone who is in the Oval Office as a result of systematic cheating, cheating organized by his own side and his own party, continue to enjoy the fruits of his bogus "victory" and impose policies—I would argue disastrous policies—that would never otherwise have been enacted?

Remember when Lance Armstrong was stripped of his Olympic medal and seven Tour de France titles after the authorities determined that he had been using illegal performance-enhancing drugs the whole time? Remember the decades-long project undertaken by various prosecutorial authorities around the world to compel the Nazis to return to Jewish families the art and valuables they stole in the 1930s? The underlying logic here is that when you steal something, whether it's art or money or athletic awards or even a presidential election, you have to return what you stole.

In this case, the Democrats stole the right of the American people to choose their own elected leader. They stole our vote. I for one want them to return what they stole, and I highly doubt that I'm alone in this sentiment. In fact, this is the sentiment of the Republican Party, or at least of a sizeable majority of the Republican Party. And if this act of restitution involves dragging the senile dotard and his cackling accomplice out of the White House, a part of me would cheer to see that happen.

Maybe it ought to happen, but will it? In July 2017, Julia Azari of the website FiveThirtyEight wrote an interesting article that explored the question of what happens if fraud determines the outcome of a presidential election. She was writing in the aftermath of the 2016 election, and the fraud she was considering was Russian interference in our presidential election. What if definitive proof emerged that Trump had colluded with Russia to defeat Hillary Clinton? What if Trump's presidency was proven to be the result of fraud?

In that case, Azari writes, there is no clear solution. "The text of the Constitution pretty much says an election is legitimate when the Electoral College says it is."[1] This view is supported by a 2016 analysis by Jack Maskell, "Legal Processes for Contesting the Results of a Presidential Election." Maskell basically concludes that once a joint session of Congress ratifies the count of the electoral votes, all legal mechanisms for objection have been exhausted.

Even Maskell's article, however, contains an interesting wrinkle. He admits that proof of significant fraud—sufficient to change the outcome of an election—throws the whole outcome into doubt, and the standard legal process out the window. Maskell invokes the "but for" standard. It's not enough to show fraud. The contestant must "prove that but for the alleged fraud or irregularity, the result of the election would have been different." Well, in this case the standard would seem to have been met.

Of course, Maskell isn't talking specifically about 2020; even so, he seems distinctly uncomfortable about where his own logic is taking him. He moves quickly to hedge his bets. "Even where the number of illegal, fraudulent, or mistaken votes is shown to exceed the margin of victory," he writes, "such showing may not, in most states, necessarily invalidate or overturn the results of the election. This is because it may be difficult for a challenger to show for whom those votes were given, or would have been given."[2]

Well, true. But if the challenger could show that those votes would almost surely have gone for him and not for the declared winner, then we have a serious problem, don't we? Maskell endeavors to shut down this line of inquiry by saying it is "unprecedented in recent American history" and that studies have shown that fraud is quite rare. Rare events do occur, however, and an unprecedented theft of a presidential election does seem to have happened in this case.

Azari's article in FiveThirtyEight cites a legal precedent that is local—a New York case in 1976—and not controlling but nevertheless quite illuminating. That year a district court in New York reviewed allegations of voter fraud in several urban locations. The court's opinion stated that federal courts had a legitimate role in ensuring free and fair elections even at the presidential level.

"It is difficult to imagine a more damaging blow to public confidence in the electoral process than the election of a President whose margin of victory was provided by fraudulent registration or voting, ballot-stuffing or other illegal means." In other words, the judge denied that presidential elections were in a sort of unique category beyond court remedy. If local and state elections can be overturned because of sufficient fraud, as has happened on several occasions, then on the same basis a presidential election presumably can be too.

In the New York case, the court rejected the allegation that there was sufficient evidence that voter fraud had altered the outcome. Yet the clear implication of the court's opinion was that if that had been the case, then the court would have been obliged to act on the matter. We know that in 2018 a congressional election was overturned and a new election held precisely because of the finding—in that case on the part of an elections board—that there had been enough fraud to tip the balance.

Even so, I must admit that the idea of removing Biden from office or redoing the 2020 presidential election now seems an unlikely outcome. For many, it will seem fanciful, and I might be called irresponsible for even raising the issue. The more likely outcome is that the powers that be in this country will go to great lengths to avoid following through on the evidence, however incontrovertible. They will seek to preserve the status quo, coming up with various explanations for why the crime of the century cannot be undone. However grave the injustice, there is no constitutional remedy. The statute of limitations has expired.

There is one remedy that the Constitution provides that has no statute of limitations. That remedy is impeachment. What this means is that a Republican Congress can begin impeachment proceedings against Joe Biden immediately upon assuming the majority. This is something that Republicans are loath to do. "Should we impeach Biden just because the Democrats twice tried to impeach Trump?" Actually, yes. Why not do to them what they have been trying to do to you? What else would make them stop?

In this case, however, there is more than sufficient reason to impeach Biden, starting with the coordinated fraud operation that his party used to put him into the White House. Was Biden aware of the fraud? This is part of a larger issue, which is whether Biden himself is aware of anything. My guess—and it's only a guess—is that many leading Democrats knew about the fraud. They knew because they were part of it.

Biden might or might not have been part of it. Quite possibly the top Democrats assured Biden that he didn't have to do much campaigning, or much of anything, because they had the whole system figured out. Biden could stay out of it because, as with his family's corrupt scheme of extracting money from foreign entities and foreign governments, the system would take care of the Big Guy.

Of course, impeachment is a very limited solution because it doesn't address the underlying point that one party—the Democratic Party—cheated its way to victory. How does getting rid of Joe Biden, even presuming this effort succeeds, solve that problem? Kamala Harris then becomes the president, even though her position is just as illegitimate as Biden's. She too was a direct beneficiary of the heist.

Let's be clear: justice requires that we have a new presidential administration; honesty requires us to recognize that Donald Trump won the election; ideally Donald Trump would be sworn in as president. It may be virtually impossible for that to happen—but that's what should happen. Joe Biden should be out, and Trump should be back in. To rectify the desecration of the 2020 election by the Democrats, the prize must go to the actual winner. Far-fetched though it may be to bring about, it's the only way to fully restore the integrity of the democratic process that was grossly and criminally corrupted in the 2020 election.

Notes

Epigraph
1. "Truth Is Incontrovertible," International Churchill Society, https://winstonchurchill.org/resources/quotes/truth-is-incontrovertible/.

Preface: Why the Truth Is So Important
1. Susie Madrak, "Morning Joe: Addressing Election Conspiracies 'Whack-a-Mole,'" Crooks & Liars, May 24, 2022, https://crooksandliars.com/2022/05/morning-joe-addressing-election.

Chapter 1: Why We Can't "Move On"
1. Randy E. Barnett, *Our Republican Constitution* (New York: Broadside Books, 2016).
2. "Remarks by President Biden to Mark One Year Since the January 6 Deadly Assault on the U.S. Capitol," The White House, January 6, 2022, https://www.whitehouse.gov/briefing-room/speeches-remarks/2022/01/06/remarks-by-president-biden-to-mark-one-year-since-the-january-6th-deadly-assault-on-the-u-s-capitol/.
3. William Cummings, "You Can Have the Election Stolen from You, Hillary Clinton Warns 2020 Democrats," *USA Today*, May 6, 2019; Bill Chappell, "Jimmy Carter Says He Sees Trump as an Illegitimate President," NPR, June 28, 2019, https://www.npr.org/2019/06/28/737008785/jimmy-carter-says-he-sees-trump-as-an-illegitimate-president.
4. See, for example, Katy Waldman, "Why We Shouldn't Talk about Normalizing Donald Trump," Slate, November 17, 2016, https://slate.com/human-interest/2016/11/stop-talking-about-normalizing-donald-trump-that-s-having-the-debate-on-his-terms.html.
5. Mollie Hemingway, *Rigged* (Washington, D.C.: Regnery, 2021), vii.
6. Catherine Kim, "Poll: 70 Percent of Republicans Don't Think the Election Was Free and Fair," *Politico*, November 9, 2020, https://www.politico.com/news/2020/11/09/republicans-free-fair-elections-435488; Max Greenwood, "Nearly Three-Quarters of GOP Doubt Legitimacy of Biden's Win: Poll," *The Hill*, December 30, 2021, https://thehill.com/homenews/campaign/587700-nearly-three-quarters-of-gop-doubt-legitimacy-of-bidens-win-poll/.

7. Jen Kirby, "Trump's Own Officials Say 2020 Was America's Most Secure Election in History," *Vox*, November 13, 2020, https://www .vox.com/2020/11/13/21563825/2020-elections-most-secure-dhs-cisa -krebs; "It's Official: The Election Was Secure," Brennan Center for Justice, December 11, 2020, https://www.brennancenter.org/our -work/research-reports/its-official-election-was-secure.

8. Justin Klawans, "Michigan Charges 3 Women with 2020 Voter Fraud, Says These 'Rare' Cases Prove Election Secure," *Newsweek*, October 11, 2021, https://www.newsweek.com/michigan-charges-3-women-2020- voter-fraud-says-these-rare-cases-prove-election-secure-1637846.

9. Brad Dress, "AP Finds Fewer than 475 Cases of Potential Voter Fraud in Six 2020 Battleground States," *The Hill*, December 15, 2021, https:// thehill.com/homenews/presidential-campaign/585901-ap-finds-fewer- than-475-cases-of-potential-voter-fraud-in-six/; "State Details of AP's Review of Potential Voter Fraud Cases," AP News, December 14, 2021, https://apnews.com/article/joe-biden-arizona-donald-trump-voter- registration-tucson-c64bba90b8c074bf8bdfd2c751b6b0f2.

10. Manu Raju, "Top Republicans Stand Up for Rounds after Trump's Attack: 'He Told the Truth,'" CNN, January 11, 2022, https://www .cnn.com/2022/01/11/politics/mike-rounds-republican-defense/index .html; Gabriel Pietrorazio, "Sen. Lindsey Graham Says 'We Could Do More in Congress and Should' to Stop Russia," ABC News, February 13, 2022, https://abcnews.go.com/Politics/sen-lindsey-graham-future-bright- gop-ahead-midterms/story?id=82850371.

Chapter 2: True the Vote

1. Christen Smith, "Ballot Harvesting Video in Pennsylvania Draws Criticism," The Center Square, October 12, 2021, https://www .thecentersquare.com/pennsylvania/ballot-harvesting-video-in -pennsylvania-draws-criticism/article_3b5be18e-2b76-11ec-9a25 -f3e5be9dbfec.html.

2. Danny Hakim and Nick Corasaniti, "Trump Campaign Draws Rebuke for Surveilling Philadelphia Voters," *New York Times*, October 22, 2020, https://www.nytimes.com/2020/10/22/us/politics/trump- campaign-voter-surveillance.html.

3. Chris Brennan, "Trump Campaign Is Warned about Videotaping Philly Voters Dropping Off Mail Ballots," *Philadelphia Inquirer*, October 22, 2020, https://www.inquirer.com/politics/election/trump-campaign- surveillance-philadelphia-mail-ballot-drop-boxes-20201022.html.

4. Todd Shepherd, "Exclusive: Trump Campaign Calls Out Mayor Kenney over 'Two Ballots' Picture," *Delaware Valley Journal*, October 23, 2020, https://delawarevalleyjournal.com/exclusive-trump -campaign-calls-out-mayor-kenney-over-two-ballots-picture/.

5. Miranda Devine, "Project Veritas Uncovers 'Ballot Harvesting Fraud' in Minnesota: Devine," *New York Post,* September 27, 2020, https://nypost.com/2020/09/27/project-veritas-uncovers-ballot-harvesting -fraud-in-minnesota/; James O'Keefe, *American Muckraker* (New York: Post Hill Press, 2022), 191–95.

6. Maggie Astor, "Project Veritas Video Was a 'Coordinated Disinformation Campaign,' Researchers Say," *New York Times,* September 29, 2020, https://www.nytimes.com/2020/09/29/us /politics/project-veritas-ilhan-omar.html; Thomas Moore, "New York Times Defends Itself against Project Veritas Defamation Suit," *The Hill,* April 13, 2021, https://thehill.com/homenews/media/547995-new-york-times-defends-itself-against-project-veritas-defamation-suit/.

7. Terri Jo Neff, "Concerned Citizens Provided FBI with Videos of Ballot Abuse, Harvesting in Yuma County," Arizona Free News, June 16, 2021, https://azfreenews.com/2021/06/concerned-citizens-provided-fbi-with-videos-of-ballot-abuse-harvesting-in-yuma-county/.

Chapter 3: What Is Geotracking?

1. True the Vote, *Election Integrity: A Citizen's Guide to Ensuring Honest Elections,* https://cdn.fs.teachablecdn.com/6nJnTKfkQ8ehBoSHE6kj.

2. "A Sampling of Recent Election Fraud Cases from across the United States," Heritage Foundation, heritage.org/voterfraud.

3. 553 U.S. 181, 128 S. Ct. 1610, 1610 (2008).

4. See, for example, Terry Golway, *Machine Made: Tammany Hall and the Creation of Modern American Politics* (New York: Liveright Publishing, 2014).

5. John Fund and Hans von Spakovsky, *Our Broken Elections* (New York: Encounter Books, 2021), 172–73.

6. Martin Tolchin, "How Johnson Won Election He'd Lost," *New York Times,* February 11, 1990, https://www.nytimes.com/1990/02/11/us /how-johnson-won-election-he-d-lost.html; David Greenberg, "Was Nixon Robbed?" Slate, October 16, 2000, https://slate.com/news-and -politics/2000/10/was-nixon-robbed.html; Josh Zeitz, "Worried about a Rigged Election? Here's One Way to Handle It," *Politico,* October 27, 2016, https://www.politico.com/magazine/story/2016/10/ donald-trump-2016-rigged-nixon-kennedy-1960-214395/.

7. Michael Graff and Nick Ochsner, *The Vote Collectors* (Chapel Hill: University of North Carolina Press, 2021).

8. Christina A. Cassidy, "Report Shows Big Spike in Mail Ballots during 2020 Election," AP News, August 16, 2021, https://apnews.com /article/health-elections-coronavirus-pandemic-election-2020-campaign-2016-f6b627a5576014a55a7252e542e46508.

9. Stuart A. Thompson and Charlie Warzel, "Twelve Million Phones, One Dataset, Zero Privacy," *New York Times*, December 19, 2019, https:// www.nytimes.com/interactive/2019/12/19/opinion/location-tracking-cell-phone.html.

10. "What You Need to Know about Location-Based Ecommerce Marketing," Campaign Creators, April 9, 2022, https://www .campaigncreators.com/blog/location-based-ecommerce-marketing.

11. Robert Windrem and Alex Johnson, "Bin Laden Aids Were Using Cell Phones, Officials Tell NBC," NBC News, May 3, 2011, https:// www.nbcnews.com/id/wbna42881728.

12. Mark Harris, "How a Secret Google Geofence Warrant Helped Catch the Capitol Riot Mob," *Wired*, September 30, 2021, https:// www.wired.com/story/capitol-riot-google-geofence-warrant/.

13. Rick Rojas, "'It's Got to Stop': Atlanta's Mayor Decries a Surge of Violence as a Girl Is Killed," *New York Times*, July 6, 2020, https:// www.nytimes.com/2020/07/06/us/atlanta-mayor-8-year-old-killed.html; Jenny Jarvie, "'You're Not Welcome Here.' The Painful Racial Reckoning Playing Out in a Wendy's Parking Lot," *Los Angeles Times*, July 15, 2020, https://www.latimes.com/world-nation/story/2020-07-15/around-the-ruins-of-a-burnt-wendys-an-atlanta -community-struggles-to-create-peace.

14. Matt McNulty, "Two 'Bloods Gang Members,' 19 and 23, Are Charged over Death of Eight-Year-Old Girl Gunned Down during BLM Riots at Atlanta Wendy's Where Rayshard Brooks Was Shot Dead by Cop," *Daily Mail*, August 13, 2021, https://www.dailymail.co.uk/news/article-9892337/2-indicted-connection-Atlanta-shooting-death-girl.html.

15. Tim Craig, "Brutal Killing of a Woman and Her Dog in an Atlanta Park Reignites the Debate over City's Growing Crime Problem," *Washington Post*, September 16, 2021, https://www.washingtonpost .com/national/brutal-killing-of-a-woman-and-her-dog-in-an-atlanta -park-reignites-the-debate-over-citys-growing-crime-problem/2021 /09/13/eae59cb2-0740-11ec-a266-7c7fe02fa374_story.html.

16. Leigh Egan, "'We Are Getting Close': Police Give Update on Atlanta Songwriter & Pet Dog Found Sliced to Death in Popular Atlanta Park," Crime Online, January 4, 2022, https://www.crimeonline.com /2022/01/04/we-are-getting-close-police-give-update-on-atlanta -songwriter-pet-dog-found-sliced-to-death-in-popular-atlanta-park/; Morse Diggs, "Piedmont Park Murder: 'A Familiarity' between Victim and Killer, Investigators Say," Fox 5 Atlanta, January 10, 2022, https:// www.fox5atlanta.com/news/piedmont-park-murder -a-familiarity-between-victim-and-killer-investigators-say.

Chapter 4: Herd of Mules

1. "Table 10: Ballot Collection Laws," National Conference of State Legislatures, May 17, 2022, https://www.ncsl.org/research/elections -and-campaigns/vopp-table-10-who-can-collect-and-return-an-absentee-ballot-other-than-the-voter.aspx; see also "Ballot Harvesting (Ballot Collection) Laws by State," Ballotpedia, https://ballotpedia.org/ Ballot_harvesting_(ballot_collection)_laws_by_state.
2. True the Vote, complaint to Georgia secretary of state Brad Raffensperger, November 30, 2021.

Chapter 5: Caught in the Act

1. Office of the Special Counsel, "Second Interim Investigative Report on the Apparatus & Procedures of the Wisconsin Elections System," delivered to the Wisconsin State Assembly on March 1, 2022.
2. Cybersecurity and Infrastructure Security Agency Elections Infrastructure Government Coordinating Council, "Ballot Drop Box," https://www.eac.gov/sites/default/files/electionofficials/vbm /Ballot_Drop_Box.pdf.
3. Paul Bond, "Film Claims It Has Video of 'Mules' Stuffing Ballot Boxes in 2020 Election," *Newsweek*, March 2, 2022, https://www .newsweek.com/film-claims-it-has-video-mules-stuffing-ballot-boxes -2020-election-1679583.

Chapter 6: An Old-School Heist

1. David Eggert, "Michigan Mails Absentee Ballot Applications to All Voters," Associated Press, May 19, 2020, https://apnews.com/article /health-elections-jocelyn-benson-voting-mi-state-wire-5ce654fb8df4d29 be57b593055cb99a6.
2. Beth LeBlanc, "Judge Rules Benson's Ballot Signature Verification Guidance 'Invalid,'" *Detroit News*, March 17, 2021, https://www .detroitnews.com/story/news/politics/2021/03/15/judge-rules-secretary-state-bensons-ballot-signature-verification-guidance -invalid/4699927001/.
3. Hans von Spakovsky, "Four Stolen Elections: The Vulnerabilities of Absentee and Mail-In Ballots," The Heritage Foundation, July 16, 2020, https://www.heritage.org/election-integrity/report/four-stolen -elections-the-vulnerabilities-absentee-and-mail-ballots.
4. Corey W. McDonald, "Developer's Conviction for Voter Fraud Reverberates throughout Hoboken," *Jersey Journal*, June 26, 2019, https://www.nj.com/hudson/2019/06/developers-conviction-for-voter -fraud-raises-questions-of-vote-by-mail-ballots-in-hoboken.html.
5. *Gooch v. Hendrix*, 5 Cal. 4th 266 (1993).

6.   "1999 Pulitzer Prizes, Journalism," The Pulitzer Prizes, https://www
      .pulitzer.org/prize-winners-by-year/1999. (The whole series of *Miami
      Herald* articles that were considered for the Pulitzer Prize are listed here.)

7.   "In Re. the Matter of the Protest of Election Returns and Absentee
      Ballots in the November 4, 1997, Election for the City of Miami, Florida,
      707 So. 2d at 1174," Third Dist. Ct. of Appeal of Florida, 1998.

8.   *Crawford v. Marion County Election Board*, 128 S. Ct. 1610 (2008).

9.   *Pabey v. Pastrick*, 816 N.E. 2d 1138 (Ind. 2004).

Chapter 7: Following the Money

1.   Molly Ball, "The Secret History of the Shadow Campaign That Saved
      the 2020 Election," *Time*, February 4, 2021, https://time.com/5936036/
      secret-2020-election-campaign/.

2.   Sasha Isenberg, *The Victory Lab* (New York: Broadway Books, 2016),
      10–11.

3.   Kirk Bado, "New Congressional Maps Reapportion Marc Elias's
      Responsibilities," *National Journal*, April 29, 2021.

4.   Marc Elias, "How to Fix Our Voting Rules before November," *The
      Atlantic*, April 5, 2020, https://www.theatlantic.com/ideas/archive
      /2020/04/how-fix-voting-right-now/609454/.

5.   Mollie Hemingway, *Rigged* (Washington, D.C.: Regnery, 2021), 20.

6.   Ibid., 37.

7.   Center for Tech and Civic Life, grant award letter to the City of
      Philadelphia, August 21, 2020. This letter was provided to the author by
      Capital Research Center, which obtained it through public records.

8.   "The Restriction of Political Campaign Intervention by Section 501(c)(3)
      Tax-Exempt Organizations," IRS, last updated September 23, 2021,
      https://www.irs.gov/charities-non-profits/charitable-organizations/the-
      restriction-of-political-campaign-intervention-by-section-501c3-tax-
      exempt-organizations#:~:text=Under%20the%20Internal%20
      Revenue%20Code,candidate%20for%20elective%20public%20office.

9.   Parker Thayer, "The Left Weaponizes Charitable Cash to Win Political
      Battles," *Capital Research*, October 2021.

Chapter 8: Looking the Other Way

1.   "Georgia Official Raffensperger: 'We Had Safe, Secure, Honest
      Elections,'" CBS News, January 10, 2021, https://www.cbsnews.com
      /video/georgia-official-raffensperger-we-had-safe-secure-honest
      -elections/.

2.   Mark Niesse, "Lawsuit Settled, Giving Georgia Voters Time to Fix
      Rejected Ballots," *Atlanta Journal-Constitution*, March 7, 2020, https://
      www.ajc.com/news/state--regional-govt--politics/lawsuit-settled-giving-
      georgia-voters-time-fix-rejected-ballots/oJcZ4eCXf8J197AEdGfsSM/.

3. John Fund and Hans Von Spakovsky, *Our Broken Elections* (New York: Encounter Books, 2021), 207.

4. Mark Niesse and Greg Bluestein, "GBI Chief: Not Enough Evidence to Pursue GOP's Ballot Fraud Claim," *Atlanta Journal-Constitution*, October 21, 2021, https://www.ajc.com/politics/gbi-chief-not-enough-evidence-to-pursue-gops-ballot-fraud-claim/YLBIKVC6OZFG7D3QIXR54UFPWU/.

5. Letter from James Bopp to Governor Brian Kemp, October 22, 2021.

6. John Solomon, "Georgia Opens Investigation into Possible Illegal Ballot Harvesting in 2020 Election," Just the News, January 4, 2022, https://justthenews.com/politics-policy/elections/georgia-opens-investigation-possible-illegal-ballot-harvesting-2020.

7. Stephen Sorace, "Georgia Secretary of State Calls for Election Reform, Says Noncitizens Should Not Be Allowed to Vote," Fox News, January 9, 2022, https://www.foxnews.com/politics/georgia-secretary-of-state-election-reform-noncitizens-voting.

8. See, for example, Van R. Newkirk II, "The Republican Party Emerges from Decades of Court Supervision," *The Atlantic*, January 9, 2018, https://www.theatlantic.com/politics/archive/2018/01/the-gop-just-received-another-tool-for-suppressing-votes/550052/.

Chapter 9: Objections and Refutations

1. "'2000 Mules': Documentary's Message Resonates with Voters," Rasmussen Reports, June 3, 2022, https://www.rasmussenreports.com/public_content/politics/public_surveys/2000_mules_documentary_s_message_resonates_with_voters.

2. Ray Stern, "Yuma County at Center of Election Conspiracies Linked to '2000 Mules' Documentary," Arizona Central, May 31, 2022, https://www.azcentral.com/story/news/politics/elections/2022/05/31/what-know-arizona-election-fraud-case-yuma-county-2000-mules/9911102002/.

3. Jerod MacDonald-Evoy, "The Yuma Sheriff Isn't Investigating Election Fraud Because of '2000 Mules,'" May 19, 2022, *Arizona Mirror*, https://www.azmirror.com/2022/05/19/the-yuma-sheriff-isnt-investigating-election-fraud-because-of-2000-mules/.

4. Danny Hakim and Alexandra Berzon, "A Big Lie in a New Package," *New York Times*, May 29, 2022, https://www.nytimes.com/2022/05/29/us/politics/2000-mules-trump-conspiracy-theory.html.

5. Philip Bump, "'Ballot Trafficking' Is the Next Front in the Unending Fight over 2020," *Washington Post*, April 6, 2022, https://www.washingtonpost.com/politics/2022/04/06/ballot-trafficking-is-next-front-unending-fight-over-2020/.

6.   Ali Swenson, "Fact Focus: Gaping Holes in the Claim of 2K Ballot 'Mules,'" Associated Press, May 3, 2022, https://apnews.com/article /2022-midterm-elections-covid-technology-health-arizona-e1b49d2311bf900f44fa5c6dac406762.

7.   Barbara Sprunt, "Here's What the Jan. 6 Panel's References to '2,000 Mules' Is About," NPR, June 13, 2022, https://www.npr.org/2022/06 /13/1104647454/jan-6-2-000-mules-trump-election.

8.   Nicco (@harambe–fren), "I keep hearing people on the left . . . ," Twitter, May 21, 2022, 7:56 a.m., https://twitter.com/harambe_fren/ status/1527981710817873921?ref_src=twsrc%5Etfw.

9.   Stuart A. Thompson and Charlie Warzel, "One Nation, Tracked: How to Track President Trump," *New York Times*, December 20, 2019, https://www.nytimes.com/interactive/2019/12/20/opinion/location-data-national-security.html; Thompson and Warzel, "One Nation, Tracked: Twelve Million Phones, One Dataset, Zero Privacy," *New York Times*, December 19, 2019, https://www.nytimes .com/interactive/2019/12/19/opinion/location-tracking-cell-phone.html.

10. Theo Wayt, "CDC Bought Cellphone Data to Track Vaccination, Lockdown Compliance: Report," *New York Post*, May 4, 2022, https:// nypost.com/2022/05/04/cdc-bought-cell-phone-data-to-track -lockdowns-vaccination-docs/; *Carpenter v. United States*, 585 U.S. ____, No.16–402 (2018), https://www.supremecourt.gov/opinions /17pdf/16-402_h315.pdf.

11. Jim Hoft, "Exclusive: Wireless Services CEO Destroys Ignorant Attacks by Fake Fact-Checkers on '2000 Mules,'" Gateway Pundit, May 26, 2022, https://www.thegatewaypundit.com/2022/05/exclusive-wireless-services-ceo-destroys-weak-attacks-fake-fact-checkers-2000-mules-fact-checkers-dont-technical-foundation-comments-making/.

12. Will Greenberg, "Data Brokers and True the Vote Are the Real Villains of '2000 Mules' Movie," Electronic Frontier Foundation, May 23, 2022, https://www.eff.org/deeplinks/2022/05/data-brokers -and-true-the-vote-are-villains-dinesh-dsouzas-latest-movie.

13. Tom Dreisbach, "A Pro-Trump Film Suggests Its Data Are So Accurate, It Solved a Murder. That's False," NPR, May 17, 2022, https:// www.npr.org/2022/05/17/1098787088/a-pro-trump-film -suggests-its-data-are-so-accurate-it-solved-a-murder-thats-fals.

14. Email from Catherine Engelbrecht to Tom Dreisbach, May 16, 2022.

15. "Discussing the Gaps in '2000 Mules' with Dinesh D'Souza," *Washington Post*, May 17, 2022, https://www.washingtonpost.com /politics/2022/05/17/discussing-gaps-2000-mules-with-dinesh-dsouza/.

16. "Fact Check: Does '2000 Mules' Provide Evidence of Voter Fraud in the 2020 U.S. Presidential Election?," Reuters, May 27, 2022, https://

www.reuters.com/article/factcheck-usa-mules/fact-check-does-2000
-mules-provide-evidence-of-voter-fraud-in-the-2020-u-s-presidential
-election-idUSL2N2XJ0OQ.

17. Swenson, "Fact Focus: Gaping Holes in the Claim of 2K Ballot 'Mules.'"
18. "Fact Check: Does '2000 Mules' Provide Evidence of Voter Fraud in the 2020 U.S. Presidential Election?," Reuters.
19. Khaya Himmelman, "Fact Checking Dinesh D'Souza's '2000 Mules,'" The Dispatch, May 21, 2022, https://thedispatch.com/p/fact -checking-dinesh-dsouzas-2000?s=r.
20. Ibid.
21. Philip Bump, "How the Falsehoods Survive," *Washington Post*, January 6, 2022, https://www.washingtonpost.com/politics/2022/01/06/how- falsehoods-survive/; Philip Bump, "'Ballot Trafficking' Is the Next Front in the Unending Fight over 2020," *Washington Post*, April 6, 2022, https://www.washingtonpost.com/politics/2022/04/06/ ballot-trafficking-is-next-front-unending-fight-over-2020/.

Chapter 10: How to Fix Election Fraud

1. Julia Azari, "What Happens If the Election Was a Fraud? The Constitution Doesn't Say," FiveThirtyEight, July 6, 2017, https:// fivethirtyeight.com/features/what-happens-if-the-election-was-a-fraud -the-constitution-doesnt-say/.
2. Jack Maskell, "Legal Processes for Contesting the Results of a Presidential Election," Congressional Research Service, October 24, 2016, https://sgp.fas .org/crs/misc/R44659.pdf.

Index